CRAZY CLIMATE AND RIGGED ECONOMIES

WE CAN DO MUCH BETTER

by

Gerry Greaves

DORRANCE
PUBLISHING CO
EST. 1920
PITTSBURGH, PENNSYLVANIA 15238

Dorrance Publishing Co
585 Alpha Drive
Suite 103
Pittsburgh, PA 15238
Visit our website at *www.dorrancebookstore.com*

ISBN: 978-1-6470-2234-1
eISBN: 978-1-6470-2892-3

CONTENTS

EXPANDED CONTENTS

PREFACE

When I was growing up, my dad had a small excavating business. As a young boy, I would sometimes hang around with him when he worked. When I was about six years old, a friend of my dad asked me what I wanted to be when I grew up. I said I wanted to build bridges.

He said, "So you want to be a construction worker."

I said, "No, I want to be the guy who designs the bridge."

He replied, "So you want to be an engineer?"

I wanted to know if that was what they called the guy who designs bridges. He confirmed it was. That was it. I wanted to be an engineer. I never wavered much from that desire. I didn't realize until much later what a blessing it was to have a clear, unwavering goal.

I did the things one does to become the guy who designs the bridge. I went to study engineering at the University of Rhode Island. Like any self-respecting college student, I wandered down a few intellectual side roads. This included chemistry, economics, and environmental engineering, but chemists, economists, and environmental engineers don't build bridges, so I became a civil engineer with an emphasis on structures.

With my freshly minted B.S., I started my career. I never did get to be the guy who designed the bridges, but I did a lot of other interesting work. I conducted structural analyses on submarine hulls. I designed composite pipes to transport water and underground storage tanks that replaced the steel tanks at gas stations. Steel tanks rusted and leaked gasoline, contaminating nearby aquifers. I dabbled in marketing (which I quickly discovered was not my life's work). I married my wonderful wife, Lisa, and we had two terrific daughters.

In the year 2000, I began my climate crisis journey. I was working in the Owens Corning Corporate Research and Development Center as an engineer on the energy-saving effects of cool roofs. Soon the discussion changed to the effect of cool roofs on the climate crisis. Cool roofs are a mild form of geoengineering, the deliberate intervention in the Earth's natural systems to counteract climate change. They reflect solar energy directly back into space and help cool the planet. I didn't know much about the climate crisis, so I did some digging. I even made a little spreadsheet climate model to get a feel for how the process worked. Even then, the scientific evidence was convincing. I came to three conclusions. First, the climate crisis was real. Second, we were causing it by emitting CO_2 from the burning of fossil fuels, and third, the effects, while uncertain, were very bad. Once one comes to these conclusions, there is a moral imperative to try to do something about it.

In my spare time, I read more about the climate crisis. I also spent some time looking at the relationship between energy and the economy. It became clear energy use and the size of the economy are highly correlated. This means when the size of the economy goes up, the energy use also goes up. I read the landmark book, *Ecological Economics, Principles and Applications,*[1] by Herman E. Daly and Joshua Farley. The hook was set. I needed to work on this.

In 2014, I retired from my career as an engineer. Although I had many reasons for deciding to retire, one of them was I had once again been blessed with a clear, unwavering goal. I wanted to try to help save the world. It sounds idealistic, ambitious, pretentious, and crazy, and it is. In my professional life, I was never a climate scientist, an economist, a policy wonk, or a writer, but I am an excellent problem solver. This is a problem worth the energy and time I have left on this earth, and yours, and of anyone who hopes for the security of future generations.

INTRODUCTION

While our understanding of climate change is not complete, the basic science is well established. The earth is warming, and most data confirms severe climate change will result. Some data questions some details of our understanding. Other data indicates change will be much worse than originally predicted. The projections of the effects are getting better all the time, and we are starting to see the impacts for ourselves. These include more severe storms, droughts, heat waves, and wildfires. It also includes sea level rise and ocean acidification. Melting glacial ice is reducing the available reserve of fresh water in many areas.

The science is increasingly clear that we are facing a serious environmental crisis. Why is it so hard to build broad support for a plan to actually do something about it? Part of the reason is the fossil fuel industry uses its considerable influence to prevent or delay action by sowing uncertainty and misinformation. Other industries and individuals with a vested interest in the status quo join in the delaying action, but there is something deeper going on. If you scratch the surface of any climate denial, you'll find three underlying assumptions. The first assumption is fixing the climate crisis would slow economic growth. The other two are the assumptions that economic growth is inherently good, and more growth is always better.

The most common metric for measuring the growth of an economy is a nation's Gross Domestic Product (GDP). Energy use correlates with GDP. When GDP goes up, energy use goes up. Energy intensity, a measure of efficiency, is the amount of energy required per unit of GDP. Studies show the energy intensity of the economy is going down as efficiency of production increases, yet it is not going down as fast as economic growth is going up, so energy use continues to increase.

Addressing the climate crisis requires converting our energy system to renewable energy sources. Because energy use correlates with GDP, we need a projection of GDP far into the future to understand the problem. Most GDP projections assume continued exponential growth. We need a projection that considers the limits we are already up against. I looked at historical data and projected it into the future with these limits in mind. The conclusion is global economic growth has been slowing since the 1960s. This is despite our best efforts to increase GDP. It is likely economic growth will approach zero by the end of this century. Lower economic growth helps mitigate climate change, but it makes income and wealth inequality worse, so to address the climate crisis we must address economic inequality at the same time.

Why is this growth slowing? Both the climate and economic systems are complex, and they closely relate to each other. We must understand the economy relies on nature's ecological systems. Ecological systems are complex and resilient, but there are limits beyond which we start to degrade them. Economic systems that worked well in an empty world are no longer appropriate for a full world. An empty world is one where we are far from the ecological limits. A full world is one where we are approaching or exceeding one or more of those limits. We are already exceeding some of the limits. For example, our burning of fossil fuels exceeds the ability of the planet to absorb our waste CO_2. The result is the climate crisis.

The ecological system is the ultimate constraint, yet there are other factors that explain why growth is slowing. For example, global population growth is slowing. This seems to be a natural occurrence in developed countries. I dig more into the population later. Education is leveling off in developed countries. This appears related to the length of human life. We can only spend so much time on education and have enough time left to reap the benefits. Productivity is also reaching a peak in developed countries. This may be a case of diminishing returns. The more productive we get, the harder it is to improve. Natural resource usage constrains the economy. All these contribute to slowing economic growth.

It's worth remembering, as we move forward, GDP is a perfectly fine measure of the size of an economy, but the size of the economy is all it measures. It does not measure the well-being of humans or anything else that exists on this planet. It only aggregates the monetary value of goods and services purchased. It counts the cost of education, sales of cigarettes, and cancer treatment exactly the same. It has nothing to say about whether these things add value to our lives.

GDP also has nothing to say about how the fruits of growth are distributed. Before talking about the distribution of wealth and income, I need to provide some perspective on the scope of my analysis. The discussion of the climate crisis is global by necessity. CO_2 emitted anywhere is quickly mixed throughout the atmosphere. The effects of the climate crisis will be different in individual countries, and the responses of individual countries will also be different. Still, the solution to the climate crisis must be global.

There are two ways to look at the distribution of wealth and income. First is the global distribution between rich and poor countries. The other is the distribution within countries. I prefer to discuss the distribution within countries because the adverse effects depend more on inequality within a country. Each country makes its own choices and solutions. This is dependent on the culture and values of the individual countries. I also focus on the United States because, as an American, I see the culture, values, and choices every day.

Research shows economic inequality in the United States is the highest among developed countries. Most Americans don't need to see the statistics to correctly sense they are not getting an equitable portion of the economic pie. As long as there have been wealthy elites, they have used their vast resources to tilt the playing field in their favor. They do this by changing the rules which define our economic system. Then they try to convince the rest of us their interests are everyone's interests.

High inequality makes a host of social maladies worse. In more equal societies, people enjoy better health and longer lives. There are fewer drug problems, obesity, mental illness, and people imprisoned, and it does not only affect the poor. The anxiety of keeping up with the Joneses or staying on top causes stress. This leads to many of these maladies.

Next, I explore global population trends and projections. While global population growth is slowing, it is quite uneven. Most developed countries have fertility rates approaching or even below the replacement rate. Many developing countries are also approaching developed country fertility rates, but Africa is a wildcard. Fertility rates in Africa are very high and coming down slowly. There is considerable uncertainty in the future of African fertility rates.

This causes uncertainty in global population projections. Better projections of African fertility rates will reduce uncertainty.

I also explore the possibility of collapse. Many isolated historic civilizations that reached the limits of their environments have collapsed, but many made better choices, adapted, and survived. They did so by reacting early with better choices. Since we are able to affect the global environment, the entire human race needs to be considered an isolated civilization. We have no outside resources on which to rely. Now, all humanity needs to react early.

The final population topic deals with age distribution distortions. Populations are getting older. This is due to the lowering of fertility rates and increasing life expectancy. This causes problems financing the care of the elderly. There are fewer working-age people to support more elderly people. This, in turn, leads to excess debt problems.

I include a discussion of debt and other constraints on the economy. Governments are generating mountains of debt. They can reduce debt in two ways: increasing taxes or reducing benefits. Due to political considerations, neither of them is popular. Debt can become excessive and destabilize the economy. To find a third way, it is important to spend some time understanding money. This is more complicated than one might think. This leads to a discussion of the inherent instability of our economic system. A discussion of campaign finance is also important. Our political campaign finance laws allow buying undue influence. The wealthy elite and large corporations use this to keep their advantages.

Whether we like it or not, this is our new reality, and we have no choice but to solve these complex, interrelated problems at the same time. Thinking of such complex interactions can be overwhelming. The good news is researchers all over the world are working on these problems. They have made significant progress in several areas.

After discussing the problems we face, I move on to suggest solutions we can choose to put in place. I begin by taking apart the three assumptions that underlie climate denial, which got us to our current predicament: fixing the climate crisis would slow economic growth, economic growth is inherently good, and more growth is always better. This worldview no longer serves us as a species. We need a new worldview to take its place. We need to adopt a worldview that recognizes when we have enough, more is not always better, and we can flourish with enough.

The picture of where we are will lead us to policy changes that can achieve the outcomes we want. Before I can do that, there needs to be a better definition of what we need. One way to think about what humans generally really need to prosper is through Maslow's hierarchy of needs: Physiological Needs (food, water, shelter, rest, etc.), Security and Safety, Belonging (intimate relationships, friends, and family), Esteem (accomplishment, recognition, prestige, etc.), and Fulfillment (purpose, achieving full potential, happiness, etc.). Maslow's hierarchy of needs has attracted criticism, yet it still rings true for many people.

In today's world, we need to add a stable and healthy environment and economy to the base of Maslow's hierarchy to support the physiological needs and security and safety as well as the higher level needs. Note that higher income is not a need. More money buys happiness only for those earning less than about twenty thousand dollars per year per person. A surprising amount of research confirms this. We start from the premise that our desired outcomes are a stable environment and fair economy rather than endless growth. Then, we can begin to choose the policies that support those priorities.

Policies to address the climate crisis are my top priority. While market economics is not a cure-all, it has proven to be an exceptionally powerful tool that uses human incentives to lead to desired outcomes. To date, emitting greenhouse gases has been essentially free. There's no cost to a power plant owner of the carbon dioxide the plant releases into the atmosphere. In fact, it would cost the owner more to put in technology to cut those emissions. Putting a price on carbon dioxide emissions ensures the costs are borne by the emitters. This harnesses the market economy to reduce carbon dioxide emissions and thus mitigate the climate crisis.

There are two key market mechanisms that have been developed to put a price on carbon. First, there is a cap and trade system. This caps the emissions and issues or auctions permits to emit. Emitters may then trade permits. The other option is a carbon emission tax, which can be revenue neutral. Either way can work, and there are advantages and disadvantages to each.

I have come to prefer a carbon tax because it is easier to get right. To be revenue neutral, proceeds from the tax can be returned to each adult citizen. For some, this will help offset the increased energy costs that result from the carbon tax. The more each individual can adjust his lifestyle to cut carbon emissions, the more of a windfall this will be. Since the wealthy use more energy than the poor, this may be considered a transfer from the rich to the poor through the government.

I will explore the global Dynamic Integrated Climate-Economy [2] (DICE) model. This is an integrated assessment model that combines simple climate and economic models. It also assesses the three critical components of any carbon pricing scheme: the effectiveness, the carbon price, and the timing.

For example, suppose we had implemented an action plan in 2015 and our goal was to stay below a 2° C temperature increase from 1900. The model suggests we could do that by applying a price of carbon emissions of $2 per ton in 2015 and gradually increase the price to $280 per ton in 2050. If such a plan had been implemented in 2015, the model predicts the atmosphere would reach a 2° C increase in about the year 2105 then start decreasing over time.

But we didn't implement carbon pricing in 2015. 2020 isn't looking particularly likely either. The model bears out what your common sense would already tell you. The longer we wait to start, the higher the required CO_2 pricing will be. Beyond that, there is a time window in which we must start. If we miss the window, we will not be able to keep the temperature increase below 2° C. It appears it is already too late to keep the temperature increase below 1.5° C.

Next, we move on to policies to address economic inequality. While the climate crisis discussion is global, the economic system and inequality discussions are focused on the U.S., but it may be applicable to other countries. We must address the rules of the economy that give advantage to the wealthy and corporations at the expense of everyone else. Some of the recommended policies allow the rules to return to the way they were thirty or forty years ago. For example, as of 2016, the United States estate tax exemption amount was $5.45 million (it increased temporarily to $11.4 million for 2019 to 2025), and the maximum rate was 40%.[64] In 1977 the estate tax exemption amount was only $460,000 in today's dollars, and the maximum rate was 70%. Returning to the 1977 law would significantly reduce economic inequality.

Other policy recommendations are new and help change the economic system to achieve desired outcomes. There are two ways to reduce inequality. First is to transfer money from the rich to the poor. The second is to provide a more equal opportunity. Either or some combination of these will provide the benefits of a more fair economy as long as inequality is reduced. In this book, you will find limited recommendations for increasing transfers to the disadvantaged.

I prefer to change the rules so the economy is fairer before transfers. This is because significantly increasing transfers seems politically impossible in the U.S. Providing equal opportunity is a fundamental value in the United States. Think of it as leveling the playing field. There are many recommendations. For each one, background information puts the recommendation in perspective.

Robert B. Reich discusses the countervailing power in his book, *Saving Capitalism, For the Many; Not the Few*.[3] The countervailing power is the aggregated power of the many to counter the power of the rich few. In extreme cases it can be violent like the American and French revolutions. In modern democracies, it is almost always political. Many proposed solutions are possible only by organizing this countervailing power. This power will be necessary to remedy inequality and the climate crisis. It was strong most recently in America from the 1930s to the early 1970s. In those years, Social Security, Welfare, Civil Rights, and economic growth all flourished. I am optimistic this countervailing power can assert itself again.

If the citizens of the U.S. were to create a countervailing power, what kinds of things should they push for to address inequality? The first goal should be to create an economy that is less subject to violent swings between expansion and recession. Expansions inflate the fortunes of the already wealthy. Recessions destroy families who are living on the edge. We can increase stability, but we shouldn't expect to smooth out all cyclical expansions and recessions.

There are several ways to make the economic system more robust and less volatile. For example, fractional reserve banking allows banks to keep only a small fraction of deposited money, currently 10% in the US. We need to constrain fractional reserve banking by increasing the reserve requirement. In our system, money is usually created by banks lending it into existence. This has caused governments, companies, and individuals to accumulate a mountain of debt. Raising the required reserve reduces individual banks' abilities to lend money into existence. Another way for the central bank to create money is through quantitative easing, the practice of buying government bonds or other financial assets in order to inject liquidity directly into the economy. It did this after the 2008 crisis. This can make up for the banks' lost abilities. The central bank can retire the government debt purchased by quantitative easing. This may be appropriate to reduce our government debt load.

Next, companies and financial institutions that are too big to fail are too big to exist. We need to break them up to provide financial stability. One last cause of financial instability is high-frequency trading on Wall Street. To further improve financial stability we must curtail this trading. We can do this by collecting a small tax on such transactions. About 0.5% to 1% of the transactions should suffice.

So far I have mentioned the size of the economy, but there is more to the story. Energy use ties the size of the economy to carbon emissions and thus to the climate crisis. To solve the climate crisis, it will be necessary to optimize the size of the economy. There is a best size of the economy based on the carrying capacity of each nation. As I mentioned previously, we are already exceeding ecological limits. As we further exceed ecological limits, economic growth will likely continue to slow. Growth is slowing even in developing countries. Sooner or later we will have to face this reality.

There are examples of civilizations that have exceeded their carrying capacity and have collapsed. Think of the collapse of the great Mayan civilization or Easter Island. In the modern world, that is likely to mean low growth, no growth, or even negative growth. Also, the economic system will become even more fragile and unstable.

The challenge will be how to thrive in these conditions. Our experience is that these conditions cause recessions and unemployment. With low growth, even the slightest perturbation will cause a recession. To avoid this, we must change the economic system to make it more resilient. This will help to avoid downturns and make surviving the ones that do happen more manageable.

From the history of collapsed, isolated civilizations, there seem to be only two options: react early or collapse. Since our isolated civilization is the whole planet, it is imperative we react early to transition to a sustainable population and a sustainable economy. First, we need to make achieving a sustainable economic scale a priority. This is a huge but critical first step. Most Americans' worldview defines economic growth as progress, and more is better. Mainstream economists have preached economic growth is the only path forward. The ultra-rich and advertisers are happy to support them. The advertising industry exists to encourage us to want things we don't need and don't make us happy for long. Challenging someone's worldview is not the best way to make friends, but we need to move to a worldview that says a sustainable economic scale is better. It will lead to more fulfilling lives and more leisure time with less stuff we don't want.

If we choose to make achieving a sustainable economic scale a priority, how do we do it? One way to manage the transition is for the central bank to have sustainable scale goals. They would keep their monetary and financial stability goals. They could reduce economic growth goals over time.

In economies with no growth, increases in productivity mean there is less work to go around. With our current economic system, this leads to unemployment. A related issue is the mountain of debt we are creating. Much of that debt is being generated to finance retirement benefits. To reduce the pressure on debt, there is currently a push to increase the standard retirement age. This increases the number of workers for a shrinking amount of work. One way around this is to increase the retirement age but reduce the standard work week. It may be possible to reduce the rigidity of the standard work week. Employees may be able to adjust their work weeks based on the situation. We must still define the details of such a system.

One final action required is to stabilize the population. A non-coercive way to do that is to make contraceptives available to anyone who wants them, globally. Another way is to make primary education available to all, globally, especially to girls. This is especially true in developing countries. Together, these steps could be enough to stabilize the population.

To get policy improvements enacted we need the support of the majority of Americans. In spite of the efforts of the fossil fuel industry and the noisiest climate deniers, most Americans think we need to address the climate crisis (58%).[115] Supporting science is becoming increasingly clear. Americans are seeing the early effects often on the evening news or on the web, and an unlucky few are feeling the impacts directly, but those passionate about it are still a minority. Similarly, many Americans believe economic inequality is a problem (64%).[116] Except for those in the higher income brackets, Americans have not seen the benefits of an expanding economy. The middle and lower classes together make up a large and passionate group as indicated by the support generated by Bernie Sanders in the 2016 election. The election of Donald Trump may also support this, but it may also be related to white identity politics or the strength of conservative media.

In any case, these very different groups may be able to form a coalition. These groups may sound like strange bedfellows, but the strongest coalitions have people who have areas where they disagree. The coalition will have to focus on the common goals of the climate crisis and economic reform. It will also have to accept or avoid areas of disagreement. These are issues that have passionate advocates but are not related to the two main goals of addressing the climate crisis and economic reform. Some issues to avoid are abortion, gay rights, race issues, gun control, health care, and Common Core. We may need to park next to people with different bumper stickers. It may be possible we will not be able to set aside our differences, but given the power and influence of the ultra-rich and fossil fuel industry, it may be our only option.

In Chapter Twelve I discuss the actions necessary to put in place the policy recommendations. First, we need to elect representatives who share the coalition's main goals. The policy recommendations I discuss may provide topics on which to correspond with your elected officials. I discuss some tips for writing to and influencing our political representatives. Also, some Non-Governmental Organizations can help influence our representatives, and supporting them may be an efficient way to gain influence with our representatives.

Finally, the conclusion in Chapter Thirteen brings all the pieces together. This completes the picture of where we are, how we can fix it, and some thoughts of how to make it happen. I provide an overview of what we covered in the book and some overarching conclusions. If I am successful, this book should help you feel comfortable with the idea that our choices can lead to better outcomes. This will allow us to construct a fairer economic system and mitigate the climate crisis, creating better lives for all.

PART I:
THE PROBLEMS

CHAPTER ONE

CLIMATE CHANGE

I'm not going to spend much time on all the data surrounding climate change. There are many excellent books on that subject. You could read Lester Brown's excellent but somewhat dated book, *World on the Edge: How to Prevent Environmental and Economic Collapse.*[4] Another good choice is Naomi Klein's, *This Changes Everything; Capitalism vs the Climate.*[5] The science of climate change is sound and the data convincing. Climate change is real. We humans are causing it by emitting CO_2 from the burning of fossil fuels, and the effects, while uncertain, are very bad. So why is it so hard for people to support doing something about it?

UNCERTAINTY

One reason for lack of public support might be the uncertainty. There are several areas of uncertainty that make people uncomfortable. I guess the two biggest are how fast is it going to get warmer, and how bad will the impacts be. The rate at which the climate gets warmer depends on what we do to mitigate it. The more we do to mitigate climate change, the slower the climate will warm. The more we do, the lower the peak temperature will be. How warm it gets determines how bad it will be. Climatologists address this uncertainty by modeling scenarios. For a given action, the models project a result. For a different action, different results are predicted. This approach provides some insight but transfers the uncertainty to what we will actually do. If we know what to do to achieve a desired result, will we have the courage to do it?

The concept of tipping points raises uncertainties about how fast the climate will change and how bad the result will be. The Merriam-Webster dictionary defines a tipping point as, "the critical point in a situation, process, or system beyond which a significant and often unstoppable effect or change takes place." Scientists have identified many potential tipping points in the climate system. Here are a few:

1. The loss of Arctic and Antarctic sea ice
2. The melting of the Antarctic and Greenland ice sheets
3. The disruption of the thermohaline circulation of ocean currents
4. Dieback of the Amazon rainforest
5. The loss of permafrost and the resulting methane (another greenhouse gas) release

We have only a limited understanding of these phenomena. The only viable way to avoid reaching one or more of these tipping points is to limit the amount of global warming. Climatologists think a 2°C increase in global average temperatures from preindustrial times is the most we can allow to avoid these tipping points. Another uncertainty is in estimating local effects. Only recently have climatologists begun to show how climate change affects regional areas. Climate models are global by necessity. Early climate models didn't have much detail. They had only a few different inputs like average land, ocean, and atmospheric temperatures, for example. Over time the resolution improved as climatologists began inputting separate land data from tropical, temperate and arctic regions. Next, they separated ocean and atmospheric data into layers and then divided large regions into smaller ones. As the models became more complex they began to depict data more representative of our planet.

Higher resolution models (working with smaller regions) require more computing time. Doubling the resolution of models requires about ten times as long to run on a given computer. Supercomputer capabilities and getting results in a reasonable time limit current models. Current climate models have regions (called cells) of about sixty by ninety miles in the middle latitudes. They have thirty layers in the atmosphere and another thirty layers in the oceans. These models are able to show expected effects on regional areas made up of several cells.

There is also uncertainty about how the oceans absorb heat from the atmosphere. The oceans absorb most of the energy the atmosphere traps, but heat flow in oceans is complex. There are currents (think of the Gulf Stream) that transport heat from the tropics to the Arctic and Antarctic poles. These currents influence the rate of heat absorption by the oceans. Global warming is reducing the temperature difference between the poles and the tropics. This weakens the currents. The amount of salt in the water also affects the currents. Melting sea ice and glaciers add fresh water to the oceans reducing salinity. This also tends to reduce the strength of the currents.

How these currents flow around the world is stable with small changes in climate, but they can become unstable with larger changes in climate (a tipping point). It is not clear how much climate change causes the currents to reorganize. Also, oceans have layers. Because temperature and salinity affect water density, the surface layer doesn't mix well with the deep ocean layers. The ocean currents also affect this mixing. The details of this are not well understood. Climatologists address these issues by making better ocean heat flow models, yet our wondrous world is very complex, and we have only limited ability to model it.

The models get better as modeling techniques improve, computers get faster, and more data becomes available. This reduces uncertainty, yet progress in science is messy and sometimes excruciatingly slow. Newton published his theory of gravity in 1687. It wasn't until 1915 that Einstein published his theory of general relativity. This showed that while Newton was not wrong, his theory was incomplete. He had an incorrect understanding of how gravity works. Scientists have tested Einstein's theory many times in different ways. The theory matches data to exquisite precision. Scientists are still trying to understand the implications of Einstein's work. Still many of our modern conveniences depend on it. Our Global Positioning System would be impossible without Einstein's work. As would accurate space trajectories (handy if you want to get to the moon). As an engineer, I have dealt with my share of messy science and uncertainty. I use the following saying to help keep it in perspective. Just because we don't know everything, doesn't mean we don't know anything.

All this uncertainty isn't the only reason it is hard for people to act on climate change. There is something deeper going on.

When we think about actually doing something about climate change, we may come to the conclusion that dealing with climate change is bad for economic growth. We come to that conclusion either on our own or by viewing news and advertising that says so. Most Americans have a worldview that says economic growth equals prosperity, so more is better. The ultra-rich and large corporations, who benefit most from growth, reinforce this thinking. It is also reinforced by recessions, which are economic contractions generally defined as two consecutive quarters of gross domestic product decline. Recessions are painful. They cause people to lose their jobs, their homes, and even declare bankruptcy. To avoid the pain of recessions in our current system, we need to do whatever we can to maintain economic growth. In the last few decades, there is a corollary to this worldview. It says anything that constrains the free market is bad.

Addressing climate change requires dramatic reductions in CO_2 emissions. The free market as it is now defined has no mechanism to do this. Converting from fossil fuels to a low carbon system requires huge investments and is likely to constrain the market and economic growth.

This challenges the common worldview and prevents us from gaining support for action. How do we get out of this conundrum? We need to think about how we define prosperity and why economic growth seems so critical. I touched on how we define prosperity in the Introduction and will look deeper at it in Chapter Six.

Our economic system has allowed us to make amazing progress in the last century, yet it has some nasty side effects. One is that it has led us to exceed ecological limits. This degrades the environment on which the economy relies. There are ways to address this, which I will discuss in later chapters. Our economic system also tends to concentrate wealth and income. This leads to economic inequality, which comes with a host of sociological problems. I will look at inequality in more detail in Chapters Three and Nine. Finally, our economic system is unstable. It is prone to boom and bust cycles and economic and financial crises. I will explore these issues in Chapter Ten.

The good news in all this is we have the power to change our economic system to meet our needs. The free market is not a free for all. It relies on a set of rules that allow it to function. These rules are not like natural laws of physics. They are rules we made and we can change. We know many of the solutions, at least in principle. The problem is our worldview prevents us from making changes that are in our own best interest. We need a different world-view. One where we have better lives, our economic system is fair, and we live within our ecological limits.

In this chapter, I have discussed my assessment of climate change. I spent some time looking at why it is so hard to accept. While I have provided some thoughts on a different worldview, it is hardly convincing at this point. I will strengthen this position throughout the rest of this book.

CHAPTER TWO

ENERGY AND THE ECONOMY

Global energy use and the size of the global economy are highly correlated. This means when GDP goes up, energy use goes up by a proportional amount. GDP is a measure of the size of an economy, and Global GDP equals the sum of the individual country GDPs. For this analysis, I obtained global energy use data that is available free on the internet from the British Petroleum Company (BP).[6]

The historical GDP data is available from the Penn World Table.[7] The University of Pennsylvania developed this data necessary to estimate historical GDP data. It is presented for individual countries. It is now administered by the University of California, Davis and the Groningen Growth Development Centre at the University of Groningen in the Netherlands. It was supplemented with recent GDP data from The World Bank.[8] The historical data is available back to 1965, so I examined the years 1965 to 2018.

I found the coefficient of determination for the correlation between energy use and GDP was 99%. This is often called R^2 (pronounced R-squared). This means one variable explains 99% of the variability in the other variable. This does not say GDP causes energy use. Correlation says only that two variables move together, not that one causes the other. Causation is much more difficult to determine. Using this data from 1965 to 2018, I was able to determine that:

Global Energy Intensity declined by about 0.69%/year.

Global Energy use increased by a factor of 3.74.

Global GDP increased by about 3.2%/year in constant dollars.

Energy intensity, in this case, is a measure of the energy needed per unit of GDP. In 2012, there was considerable discussion of decoupling energy use from GDP in the U.S. Energy use per GDP dollar in the U.S. provides some evidence to support decoupling. Over the period 1965 to 2018 the US energy intensity fell at a rate of about 1.7% per year. If this trend continued at that rate, we would soon be making everything with no energy at all. Okay, it wasn't quite that bad, but there was a belief the economy was fundamentally changing.

The economy was changing, but the change was greater than energy efficiency improvements could explain. The discussion was more about the U.S. moving from heavy industry to a service economy. For example, products like computer programs require almost no energy after the initial development. They are not even shipped. We download them from the internet.

Improving energy efficiency reduces energy intensity, and in a way, this can be seen as a method of decoupling energy use from GDP. For example, think of a cab driver back in the 1960s. The money the cab driver receives is part of the GDP. He would have had to spend a lot of money on gas for his cab. Remember, this was the 1960s when everyone drove some version of a gas-guzzling behemoth. Say he had a relatively efficient behemoth that got twelve miles per gallon of gasoline. Today, cars are much more energy efficient, and a cab driver might drive a Toyota Prius and get fifty miles per gallon. So in the 1960s, the cab driver's energy intensity was about eighty-three gallons of gasoline per one thousand miles. In today's Prius, the cab driver's energy intensity is about twenty gallons of gasoline per one thousand miles.

Since the 1.7% decline in energy intensity didn't make sense, I suspected international trade had something to do with it. The global energy intensity, which fell at a rate of 0.69% per year, was not coming down nearly as fast as the U.S. energy intensity. The implication is we are importing some of our energy disguised as high energy-intensive products like steel. If this is true, decoupling was not as big as it appeared, yet one could argue the U.S. was decoupling energy use from GDP and the rest of the world would catch up over time. To some extent that is also true. What conclusions can we draw from this?

Over the period from 1965 to 2018, the U.S. GDP grew at about 2.9% per year while energy intensity declined at about 1.7% per year, yet our energy consumption was still increasing, in fact, by about 1.2% per year. Our improvements in energy efficiency and economic transformation were not keeping up with our energy use. We were in no danger of producing everything without any energy at all.

Globally, the story is similar. Over the period from 1965 to 2018, energy consumption was increasing faster than the global economy was decoupling. In fact, energy consumption went up by about 2.5% per year while GDP grew by 3.2% per year and energy intensity fell by about 0.69% per year.

Next, let's take a look at energy use. If energy use continues to grow at about 2.5% per year, then energy use in the year 2100 could be over 6 times the energy use in 2018. The chance of the world being able to supply this much energy from low carbon sources or otherwise is not good. Of course, this projection was done with an exponential function, and assumed a constant percentage increase each year.

There are several ways to mathematically predict future conditions by projecting available historical data. Such projections are normally done by choosing a form of an equation and fit that equation to the data. To fit an equation means to determine the best constants in the equation so it best matches the data. Then that equation is used to project the data into the future.

As stated above, I chose to use an exponential function to project energy use. The particular function used is often called the form of an equation. An exponential function describes a constant percentage increase per year. If I had used a quadratic function, projected energy use in 2100 could be about 3 times our 2018 energy use. Using a linear function, energy use in 2100 would be about 2 times our 2018 energy use. This highlights an important point in projecting data. The form of the equation used to project the data matters.

So how does one choose the best form of the equation? The first way is to compare the coefficient of determination (R^2) among the choices. Unfortunately, in this case, the coefficients of determination for all three choices (exponential, quadratic, and linear) are about equal. In the physical sciences, it is possible to choose the function based on first principles or, in other words, the laws of physics. However, once people are involved, the laws of physics offer little guidance. There are no such laws in the social sciences, yet we know energy use is correlated to GDP. So if we can project GDP, we can use that to find the best form of the equation to project energy use. I project GDP in the next section and use that to project energy use.

PROJECTION OF HISTORICAL GLOBAL ECONOMIC GROWTH

I was able to squeeze another bit of information from the GDP data. Let's look at the global data. Over the period from 1965 to 2018, global GDP grew by about 3.2% per year. Of course, it was not 3.2% every year. It bounces around quite a bit, but there is also a trend toward slower growth. We can smooth it a little by using a five-year moving average, and the trend becomes clearer. We can smooth is some more by using a ten-year moving average and the trend becomes clearer still. To give you a feel, here are the numbers by decade [8].

Decade	Global GDP Growth %/year
1961–1970	5.4
1971–1980	3.8
1981–1990	3.2
1991–2000	2.8
2001–2010	2.8
2011–2018	2.4

Table 2.1. Global GDP growth by decade.

What is causing this slowing of global economic growth? What does this say about projecting GDP into the future?

Before digging into some of the factors affecting economic growth, I will explore GDP a bit more. I will use a form of the equation that is often used in population projections. First, let's see what other GDP data is available. Over longer periods, the GDP data gets pretty scarce. Still, there have been some estimates back 2000 years.[132] The long-term data does show some interesting trends. For a long time (say year 1 to about 1700) not much happened. There was very slow, almost linear growth. Then at about 1700, GDP began to take off.

The exact changing point is difficult to discern. It is about the time of the industrial revolution (generally 1760–1840). From then on, economic growth increased rapidly. If you plot GDP versus time, the plot will curve upward.

This appeared to be the case until about the 1960s. After that, the economic growth percent increase began to drop as shown in Table 2.1. From the 1960s to the present linear growth is a better fit, but only a little better. How well does an exponential equation fit the data?

Using the whole data set for the last 2000 years, the exponential form doesn't fit the data well at all. It significantly over-predicts before about 1700. Then from about 1700 to 1960, it under-predicts. Finally, after 1960 it over-predicts again. The exponential form can fit part of the data a little better. Starting in 1820 (a year an estimate is available), it is better but still not re-sponsive enough. The exponential form has problems representing the indus-trial revolution. Also, it is starting to not fit the last few decades that well. It appears it is not the best form.

There is a family of forms called sigmoid functions.[11] These are "S" curves. They start horizontally at some level (often zero) then at some point curve up-ward toward a mid-point. After that, they start to curve in the other direction back toward horizontal at a higher level. Depending on the parameters, the middle section often appears linear. There is a particular sigmoid function called the logistic function.[12] This function defines the sigmoid with three pa-rameters. The first is the midpoint on the horizontal axis. The second is the maximum on the vertical axis. The third is the steepness of the curve at the midpoint. I am trying hard to avoid equations in this book, but sometimes they seem appropriate. I will explain the implications of any equations used. I show the equation for the logistic sigmoid function below.

$$f(x) = \frac{L}{1 + e^{-k(x-x_0)}} \tag{2.1}$$

Where,
   $f(x)$ = the variable of interest, for example, GDP,
   e = the natural logarithm base (also known as Euler's number),
   x_0 = the x-value of the sigmoid curve midpoint, for us this will be time, in years,
   L = the curve's maximum value,
   k = the slope or steepness of the curve.

An early application of this function was to understand population growth. Pierre-François Verhulst used it in 1838 to model population growth. Since then it has been useful in modeling many types of growth. It is also useful in other types of problems, including chemical reactions and crop responses to various inputs. Using the logistic function on our global GDP data, it fits the whole set of data very well. Fitting involves determining the three parameters that best match the data. It turns out, for global GDP, the best fit midpoint is the year 2012, and the maximum is about 2.12 times where we were in 2018. This is an extraordinary claim. It says there will be only one more doubling of the size of the economy.

The logistic function seems to fit the data well, but to believe it, we need more support. From Verhulst, a logistic function seems to model the population well. Population contributes to GDP, so it makes sense GDP may also follow a logistic curve, yet one problem is that we appear to be near the midpoint. It takes a leap of faith to assume things are going to start off in a different direction when it is only suggested by the data.

In simple economic growth models, economic output (GDP) depends on three factors. These are population (labor), capital stock, and something called the total factor productivity. The total factor productivity is best thought of as a measure of the level of technology. A workhorse model of macroeconomics is the Solow[9] model. It was developed by Bob Solow (and independently by Trevor Swan) in 1956. It has shaped the whole field of macroeconomics. Acemoglu dedicates a chapter in his book on economic growth to discussing it.[13] It is remarkable in its simplicity, power, and extendibility.

I will explore one of the extensions later. For my purpose now of exploring why economic growth is slowing, I use the basic form below in Equation 2.2.

$$Y = A K^\alpha L^{(1-\alpha)} \tag{2.2}$$

Where,

 Y = the economic output or GDP per year,
 A = the total factor productivity,
 K = the capital stock,
 α = the output elasticity of the capital stock (often assumed to be about 0.3), and
 L = the population.

This shows how the individual factors (productivity, capital stock, and population) are combined to calculate GDP. I used the individual factors to understand why the global GDP growth is slowing. The slowing of population growth is contributing to slowing global economic growth. I will examine population issues some below and have a broader exploration in Chapter Four.

Projecting the individual factors and developing an improved version of the Solow into a model is pretty technical and involves lots of equations. I used this improved version of the Solow model, sometimes called the Mankiw–Romer-Weil model, to project GDP. If you are mathematically inclined or just interested, it is discussed in the Appendix. Table 2.2 below shows the global GDP growth per decade with projections to 2200 from this model.

Decade	Average Annual Global GDP Growth, %
1961–1970	5.4
1971–1980	3.8
1981–1990	3.2
1991–2000	2.8
2001–2010	2.8
2011–2020 projection	2.7
2021–2030 projection	2.1
2031–2040 projection	1.6
2041–2050 projection	1.1
2051–2060 projection	0.8
2061–2070 projection	0.5
2071–2080 projection	0.3
2081–2090 projection	0.2
2091–2100 projection	0.1
2141–2150 projection	0.0
2191–2200 projection	0.0

Table 2.2. Projection of annual global GDP growth by decade, using the Mankiw–Romer-Weil model.

When I first made this table, it stunned me. I had been plotting global GDP and the various factors. They showed economic growth was slowing and GDP would eventually level off, but putting numbers into that table still gave me pause. This trend is not something that is far in the future; it started decades ago, and it is unfolding before our eyes.

With our current economic system, slowing economic growth has sobering implications for inequality. Thomas Piketty made this very clear in his 2014 tome, *Capital in the Twenty-First Century*.[16] A basic premise of his book is that when the return on capital is greater than the economic growth rate, inequality of wealth increases. This implies those who have money can increase their wealth faster than those who don't. That increases the inequality of wealth.

It may be helpful to think of the case where there is no economic growth. In that case, the economy becomes a zero-sum game. That means if I get richer, someone else must get poorer. If I consume more, someone else must consume less. Inequality will be discussed more in Chapter Three. Modifying our economic system to make it fairer will be discussed in Chapter Nine, but now let's get back to the discussion of energy.

With the Mankiw–Romer–Weil model, it is now possible to make a better projection of GDP and our energy needs for the year 2100 and beyond. When I look at long-term climate and the economy, I usually go out to the year 2300. The integrated assessment model discussed more in Chapter Eight also extends to the year 2300. It is beyond when the economic model discussed above approaches its maximum, so I will project our energy use to the year 2300.

Projecting energy use requires a projected energy intensity. Plotting energy intensity versus time shows a nice downward sloping set of data, yet a linear curve fit line crosses zero in about the year 2100. This, of course, is impossible. We can't generate GDP with zero or negative energy use. It is possible to use an exponential curve fit, which fits the data about as well as a linear fit. This results in a curve that asymptotically approaches zero.

Now, I can multiply the projected energy intensity times the projected GDP to project energy use. This yields some surprising results. The combination of lower growth and lower energy intensity results in a projected energy use maximum in about the year 2050. This maximum is only about 15% higher than it was in 2016. By the year 2300, the projected energy use is only 20% of the value in 2016. The projected energy intensity is only 9% of what it was in 2016. Can this be true?

The energy use maximum happens when economic growth is less than the reduction in energy intensity. Can we continue to reduce energy intensity by the same percentage until 2050 and beyond? There is nothing in the data to suggest we can or we cannot. There are ample opportunities for energy efficiency improvements in buildings and transportation. As economies continue to become more service-oriented, their energy intensity will drop.

Continuing to reduce energy intensity at current rates on a percentage basis for thirty years seems reasonable. Whether we can do it for 281 years to 2300 is another question, but that too may be possible. Doing so violates no laws of physics. As the GDP reaches a maximum, there will be less need to build and manufacture stuff. The economy will tend to be service dominated with lower energy intensity, so it can be true. In almost three hundred years, we can make unimaginable improvements in energy efficiency. The economy can transform into something unrecognizable.

How confident should we be about these projections? We should be pretty confident about reductions in energy intensity for the next several decades. We can even have some confidence for the rest of this century. The pieces are already in place.

The most efficient hybrid automobiles are much more efficient than the current average. We can replace the existing automobile stock with new models over the next few decades. Beyond that, electric automobiles are the next wave of automobile efficiency improvements. We can power these with renewable energy. It may take a couple of decades to improve battery technology enough. Many of these technologies will be translatable to trucks as well. Self-driving cars can improve efficiency by improving traffic flow. Finally, better use of electric trains and subway systems will reduce the need for cars. This can also reduce the need for cars and planes for intermediate distance travel. Lighter, stronger materials are becoming more common in all these vehicles. This makes them more efficient. It's not hard to imagine these improvements in efficiency taking place in this century.

There is a similar story for building energy efficiency. Over the last sixty years, there have been tremendous improvements in building technologies. These improve energy efficiency but also air quality and comfort. I spent much of the last fifteen years or so of my career improving the energy efficiency of homes. Some major builders are even building zero-energy homes in some areas. Zero-energy homes are homes that, over a year, produce as much energy as they use.

This is accomplished by improving all aspects of energy use in the home. This includes everything from the building envelope to equipment and lighting. The building envelope is the part of the building that keeps the inside in and outside out. The building envelope includes walls, roofs, windows, and doors. Reducing heat flow and air flow through the building envelope improves efficiency.

All the equipment is available in a range of efficiencies. This includes HVAC equipment, water heaters, and appliances. HVAC equipment is heating, ventilating, and air conditioning equipment. Designing a zero-energy home involves improving all these features. This continues until the cost of more improvements is more than the cost of the energy saved. The cost of the energy is determined by the cost of putting photovoltaic solar panels on the roof. The dominant home design will most likely be a zero-energy home without the solar panels. It will have electricity provided by the grid from renewable sources. Similar improvements have been made in commercial buildings. Improving existing buildings is difficult and expensive. Buildings have much longer lives than cars. Converting our building stock to high-efficiency buildings will take several decades. Again, it's not hard to imagine this taking place in this century.

Finally, as economic growth slows, the need for high energy-intensive materials like steel, aluminum, and cement will slow. This will further reduce the energy intensity of the economy. So it is easy to imagine our rate of energy intensity reduction will continue for the rest of this century. After that, it becomes difficult to imagine how this will happen, but it doesn't appear impossible either. This century is where we must make the important choices.

How confident should we be in the economic model? Mainstream economists come to a quite different conclusion. These economists project continued exponential GDP growth into the future. This is not consistent with the data from the last six decades. It is difficult to imagine it continuing for the rest of this century without running into environmental limits. It has not even been happening for the last six decades.

There are two different economic approaches used to project future conditions. One is to develop theories based on explaining the available data. The other is to develop internally consistent and elegant theories. Internally consistent means none of the assumptions or predictions conflict with other assumptions or predictions of the model. This is often done with little regard for the data. Great economists generally choose one of these approaches.

Landreth and Colander discuss this in *History of Economic Thought*.[17] Over the last few centuries, the pendulum has swung back and forth from one to the other. Over the last few decades, the internally consistent theories approach has been dominating. This helps to explain why most economists missed the great recession of 2008 and 2009.

I am firmly in favor of developing theories based on explaining the available data. As an engineer, I worked almost my entire career in research and development. Over the years, I became known as an excellent problem solver. I collected various problem-solving tools. These included statistical analysis, team building tools, and generic problem-solving tools, but my best tool was to follow the data wherever it led. Sometimes it led to uncomfortable places, but my approach was to find the truth and then find a way to deal with it.

I also tended to bring together information from various sources then assemble them into a coherent understanding of the problem. For the last seven years before I retired, I worked in our company's sustainability department. I put most of these tools to use to explore the energy, climate change, and the economic problems in my spare time. Since my retirement, I have been able to focus more on these problems. Climate change combined with economic inequality rank among the most difficult problems with tendrils going off in several directions, but I enjoy solving problems, and this is putting my problem-solving skills to the test.

I read a bookshelf full of books on basic economics, the history of economic thought, business cycles, climate change, modern economic growth theories, ecological economics, the collapse of ecological systems, and wealth and income inequality. I set off to try to find as much data as I could and try to make sense of it. I found a wealth of economic and energy data available for free on the internet. Finally, I was able to use my newfound understanding and data along with my old problem-solving tool kit to build a model to project GDP and energy use. I used my follow the data paradigm. The result was the model discussed in this chapter.

I am confident the future will look something like what the model is showing us, but don't get too caught up on the exact timing I discussed. My understanding is incomplete as is the available data. Mainstream economists will most likely dismiss this approach. They will claim someone not schooled in economics can't understand. To them I reply the data is from reliable sources, and my analysis is sound. Perhaps their understanding is also incomplete.

I suspect some future historian will look back at the twenty-first century and label it as a century of transition. This is a transition much like the one from adolescence to adulthood. I am hopeful it will be a transition to a better world. I must admit on some days I throw up my hands and think we are doomed, but on most days, I am optimistic eventually we will make the right choices.

CHAPTER THREE

INEQUALITY

In the last chapter, I showed how economic growth has been slowing for six decades. It appears it will continue to slow and eventually stop growing. In the 1960s, an aphorism became popular that said, "A rising tide lifts all boats."[18] The phrase is often attributed to President Kennedy. Though JFK used it often, neither he nor his speechwriter, Sorensen, originated it. As they used the saying, it means economic growth benefits all. While it may apply well to boats, in recent decades it has not been a good descriptor of economic conditions for the general population. In the U.S. in the last forty years, economic growth has benefited the wealthy much more than it has the middle class. In fact, the real income (adjusted for inflation) of the middle class has hardly budged. Many Americans in the middle class feel they are not getting their fair share. They are right. Most of the income of an expanding economy goes to the wealthy. The disgruntled middle class is a large and passionate group. The election of Donald Trump and the support generated by Bernie Sanders supports this, but President Trump's support may also be related to white identity politics or the strength of conservative media. In any case, with economic growth slowing, even the pretext of the rising tide aphorism is no longer viable.

Over this forty-year period, inequality as measured by the Gini Coefficient has increased in the U.S. and, in most countries, in the Organization for Economic Co-operation and Development (OECD). The OECD is a club of developed countries. The Gini Coefficient indicates how equal a county's income (or wealth) distribution is. It is the most often used measure of inequality. It ranges from 0 where everyone has the same income (or wealth) to 1 where one person has all the income (or wealth). Income inequality can be either disposable income or market income. Disposable income is after taxes and transfers like social security and welfare. Market income is before taxes and transfers.

In the U.S. in the mid-1970s, the Gini Coefficient was 0.406 for market income and 0.316 for disposable income. By 2014, those numbers had gone up to 0.486 for market income and 0.378 for disposable income.[19] Of the thirty-four countries in the OECD, the U.S. now has the fourth highest inequality. Only Turkey, Chile, and Mexico are higher.

Is inequality bad for society and us as individuals? The short answer is it depends on how much. Those who argue inequality is good[20] say getting rich is the reward for taking business risks. It is these risks that drive innovation and economic growth and thus "lift all boats." Taken to the extreme, this logic means more inequality is better. The logical endpoint of such reasoning would conclude an income Gini Coefficient of 1 should be best of all, but an income Gini Coefficient of 1 means one person has all the income. That can't be good.

What about the other extreme of an income Gini Coefficient of 0 where everybody has the same income? This has been one of the goals of Utopian societies for ages. The problem is, while many have tried, none have succeeded on any significant scale. If everyone has the same income, there is little or no incentive to seek a job with more responsibility, a managerial or leadership position, for example. Most people need some form of incentive to work. Earning money to provide for themselves and their families is a major incentive. Other incentives might include the interaction and camaraderie with workmates or the challenges and rewards of success and achieving their potential, but for most people, if they didn't get paid what they think they are worth, they are unlikely to do their best.

There is likely an optimum level of inequality. One way to get a handle on that is to ask people how much equality they want. This has already been done by Dan Ariely and presented in 2015 in a TED talk: "How equal do we want the world to be. You'd be surprised."[21] For more interesting TED talks, see a blog I wrote for the Post Growth website. It is, "Equality in a post-growth society: Are we ready for tomorrow?"[22] In this chapter, I will be expanding on some of that material. Dan Ariely asked about wealth inequality, but it can provide some insight on income inequality as well. He asked more than five thousand Americans how much of the nation's wealth should go to each fifth of the population. For example, how much should the richest fifth or the poorest fifth have? He was a little tricky in the way he asked, in that he told them to assume they would not know which fifth they would be born into in this hypothetical society, so they would answer without knowing which fifth they would be in. I show the results below along with the actual U.S. distribution and an example that is based on a Gini Coefficient of 0.55 like Japan.

Group	Percent of wealth desired [21]	U.S. wealth data	Example
Bottom 20%	10.5%	0.1%	3%
Second 20%	14.1%	0.2%	5%
Third 20%	21.5%	3.9%	8%
Fourth 20%	22.0%	11.3%	19%
Top 20%	31.9%	84.4%	65%
Gini Coefficient	0.20	0.77	0.55

Table 3.1. Desired, US and Example wealth distributions.

There are several things to be learned from this table. First, Ariely's subjects chose neither perfect equality nor perfect inequality. Next, note their desired distribution is far from the U.S. actual data. The distributions above have approximate Gini Coefficients of 0.20 desired versus 0.77 for the US data. The next question I had is how likely are we to be able to achieve the desired wealth distribution. I looked for the OECD country with the lowest wealth Gini Coefficient. It turns out to be Japan with a wealth Gini Coefficient of 0.55. This tells us we are not likely to achieve the wealth Gini Coefficient of 0.2 Ariely's study concluded. The example in the table has a wealth Gini Coefficient of 0.55 like Japan. If we want to lower the U.S. wealth Gini, 0.55 may be an appropriate goal.

Taking a similar approach to income inequality, I looked for the country with the lowest Gini Coefficient for income. I prefer disposable income because it better represents inequality. It turns out Slovenia has the lowest disposable income Gini Coefficient of 0.236 compared to the US at 0.378. For an example, with a larger economy, I would choose Denmark at 0.248 or Germany at 0.295. The OECD country with the greatest disposable income Gini Coefficient is Mexico at 0.476. It is far above second place Turkey at 0.405.

There are two ways to affect these Gini Coefficients. One way is to redistribute income and wealth after it is earned. This can be done by using progressive tax rates whereby higher income or wealth is taxed at a higher rate than lower income or wealth. It may also be done by using transfers such as welfare, social security, or unemployment benefits. Think of this as providing a safety net. The other way to affect these Gini Coefficients is to change the rules by which the economy runs. Think of this as creating a more level playing field. Our economic system is based on rules that we chose through our government. The U.S. system has many rules that favor those with wealth and power. The ultra-rich use their political power to ensure this is so. Other countries have made different choices and have achieved different results. We in the U.S. can also make other choices to achieve lower Gini Coefficients.

Data is available for both the market and disposable income Gini Coefficients. I looked at how different countries achieved their disposable income distributions. I have chosen a few countries as examples. Table 3.2 below shows Gini Coefficients for market income, disposable income, and the difference between the two. It also shows some statistics for the whole group.

Description	Market	Disposable	Difference
South Korea	0.344	0.315	0.029
Denmark	0.416	0.248	0.168
Germany	0.504	0.295	0.209
Mexico	0.494	0.476	0.018
United States	0.486	0.378	0.108
Minimum OECD	0.344	0.236	0.018
Average OECD	0.454	0.310	0.142
Maximum OECD	0.534	0.476	0.211

Table 3.2. Market income Gini Coefficients, Disposable income Gini Coefficients, and the difference between them for selected countries along with the minimums, averages, and maximums of the OECD countries.

The lowest market income Gini Coefficient belongs to South Korea. It has a disposable income Gini Coefficient that is a little above the average and a difference that is second lowest. This suggests South Korea has chosen to focus on creating a level playing field. It provides minimal transfers. Denmark has below average market and disposable income Gini Coefficients. It also has an above average difference. This suggests Denmark has chosen to level the playing field and provide a safety net. By contrast, Mexico has a high market income Gini Coefficient and the highest disposable income Gini Coefficient. It also has the lowest difference. Mexico has chosen neither to level the playing field nor provide a safety net. Germany has a high market Gini Coefficient and a below average disposable Gini Coefficient. It has the second highest difference. This suggests Germany has chosen to focus on the safety net. Finally, the United States has the sixth highest market income Gini Coefficient and the fourth highest disposable income Gini Coefficient. It has a below average difference. This suggests the United States has chosen to do little to either level the playing field or provide a safety net. This highlights how different countries have chosen different responses to inequality.

This raises two questions. First, is lower inequality worth the significant effort to achieve it? This requires the many to challenge the ultra-rich few to make the required changes. Second, exactly what changes should we make? I will discuss the many advantages of a fairer economic system below. I discuss the changes I think are needed in Chapter Nine.

The Spirit Level,[23] by Richard Wilkinson and Kate Pickett, summarizes the authors' work on inequality. They compared various measures of societal health for different countries. They compared twenty-one countries with different levels of inequality. They also looked at the fifty U.S. states, which have quite varied levels of inequality. In both cases, more inequality resulted in worse social maladies. In 2010, the Center for the Advancement of the Steady State Economy (CASSE) sponsored the Steady State Economy Conference. *Enough is Enough*[24] reports the results of that conference and summarizes the benefits of more equal societies very well:

1. People enjoy better health and a higher life expectancy;
2. Fewer citizens have drug problems;
3. People are less victimized by violence;
4. Teenage birth rates are lower;
5. Children experience higher levels of well-being;
6. The rate of obesity is lower;
7. Mental illness is less common;
8. Many fewer people are imprisoned; and
9. Opportunities for social mobility are more widespread.

This summary is a remarkable list. *The Spirit Level* authors demonstrated a correlation between the level of inequality and each item on the list. Lower inequality was associated with better outcomes both among countries and among U.S. states. The authors claim inequality causes worse outcomes. Of course, proving causality is difficult, but the authors make a strong case. A *Scientific American* article "The Health-Wealth Gap"[25] supports the claim of causality. It provides the results of physical, neurological and psychological tests. These results are worse with higher inequality.

Another *Scientific American* article, "The Environmental Cost of Inequality"[26] also supports the causality. Inequality causes poor environmental outcomes. The mechanism goes something like this: The benefits of degrading the environment go to the wealthy and large corporations. The costs often go to the poor. This is because the wealthy and large corporations have more economic and political power. This difference is bigger in more unequal societies, so greater inequality allows for greater environmental degradation. This supports the claim that inequality causes bad outcomes. If this causality is true, we can improve all these maladies by reducing inequality.

One concept these articles discussed that struck me is that of status anxiety. Think of this as worrying about keeping up with the Joneses. A little different version is worrying about getting ahead of the Joneses, and this is not just an issue for the poor. It affects all levels of society. Each level worries about keeping on their step of the social status ladder or moving up. Even people at the top obsess about staying there. Of course, not everyone reacts this way, but many people do. In more unequal societies, that anxiety can lead to worse outcomes. In today's societies, almost everyone has access to view the lifestyles of the rich and famous. The pressure and anxiety can be overwhelming.

The Spirit Level also finds it doesn't matter how societies achieve less inequality. It only matters that they do. In the discussion above, I mentioned two ways to lower inequality. The first is leveling the playing field. The second is providing a safety net. Different countries did it one way or the other or some combination of the two. This finding says it doesn't matter how we reduce inequality. Each country can make their own choices based on their own cultures and preferences.

In the United States, we have a strong preference for individuality and self-sufficiency. We also have distaste for things that might look like a handout. We do have safety nets in the form of social security, welfare, and food stamps. While we could simplify and update the safety net, this seems to be the most we are likely to be able to achieve. Still, our level of inequality is too high by developed nation standards, and we seem to be paying the price. Our playing field is too tilted in favor of the wealthy. Leveling the playing field is an area where there is much we can do and still be consistent with our culture. I will discuss those in Chapter Nine.

Chapter Four

Population

Global Population

There are several things to discuss concerning the population. I will start with a discussion of the world's total population. In 2016, there were 7.4 billion of us. The 2019 projections from the United Nations go to the year 2100. They project an average population of 10.9 billion in the year 2100 with 95% confidence limits of 9.6 to 13.2 billion. The logistic curve fit from Chapter Two suggests an average of 11.4 billion in 2100. The sheer number of us the U.N. expects in the year 2100 is noteworthy. There will be from 2.2 to 5.8 billion more than today. It is doubtful the earth will be able to produce enough food for that many people without depleting the necessary natural resources. These resources include fresh water, soil, and fertilizer. We are already using more water than is being replenished, lowering aquifer levels. Climate change means less snowpack and glacier ice in the mountains to provide meltwater in the summer. Our soils are being eroded and washing down rivers. One of the key ingredients in fertilizer is mined phosphate, which is being depleted. Also, there is already a massive runoff of excess fertilizer that is polluting our rivers. Where these rivers empty into oceans they cause dead spots, and red tide algae blooms.

Still, there are reasons for hope. There is a tremendous amount of waste in our food supply system. This includes waste in production, distribution and use systems. Much of the water we use for irrigation never reaches plants. It ends up evaporating or as runoff, carrying soil and fertilizer with it down rivers and into oceans. Better technologies exist. No-till farming and drip irrigation can reduce these wastes. Real-time monitoring of key variables can allow water and fertilizer application only when and where needed. The use of these technologies is growing, but they are still only used on a small percentage of the world's arable land. A significant amount of food spoils in the distribution and storage systems. In developing countries, much of the spoilage is due to inadequate infrastructure such as unrefrigerated trucks and storage facilities. Distribution and storage are much better in developed countries.

In the U.S., we have come to expect perfect produce. Grocers throw out produce with minor blemishes because they know it won't sell. It is not clear how to resolve this. It may be that education will be able to alter our buying habits. It may be we will learn to be less discriminating buyers if blemished produce is all that is available. Finally, we throw out a significant amount of food because it goes bad before we can eat it. Think of your own refrigerator. Food gets thrown out because we bought too much or leftovers don't get eaten. Again, I'm not sure we can improve this. In any case, there are many ways to improve the efficiency of our food supply system. In some areas, we may need to change our habits, but change is likely to be slow. In other areas, the technologies already exist. We need to use them more. It is difficult to predict how fast this may happen.

Another way to ease the pressure on the food supply is to change our eating habits. Most people in developed countries eat more meat than is healthy. It takes about six pounds of grain to produce one pound of beef. Chicken takes about 2.5 pounds and pork is about 3.5 pounds of grain per pound of meat.[131] While there is some controversy around these numbers, the bottom line is that people in developed countries eat a lot of meat. The average American eats about 270 pounds of meat per year. Of course, that is not common around the world. If you are an average person from Bangladesh you eat 4 pounds per year. Globally we eat about 124 million tons of poultry, 91 million tons of pork, 59 million tons of beef, and 11 million tons of other meat.[27] This is a grand total of 285 million tons of meat per year. Producing all that meat consumes 1.3 billion tons of grain or about 4.6 pounds of grain per pound of meat. Globally, it is 77 pounds of meat per person per year. It is safe to say eating less meat would be healthier for many people and the planet and leave it at that.

UNCERTAINTY

Another point to notice about the U.N. population projection is the uncertainty. The latest U.N. projection predicts a world population of 11.4 billion in the year 2100. The 95% confidence limits are 9.6 to 13.2 billion. In 2004 the U.N. projected world population to the year 2300. The medium projection was nine billion in the year 2300. They gave low and high projections of 2.3 to 36.4 billion. What could cause such a wide range?

Population projections often make three sets of assumptions: fertility, mortality, and migration.[28] The U.N., of course, does a very thorough job of making its projections. For the 2017 projection, it broke the world population into 233 countries and regions. Then it broke each of those into five-year cohorts and by sex. A five-year cohort is a group of people in the same five-year age group. For example, a group of females aged six to ten years. For each cohort in each country or region and sex, it made projections for mortality and migration and fertility for females. It then projected populations for each combination. Finally, it added up all the countries and regions. This produced a projection of the total population. It also projected the number of people in each cohort, sex, and country.[29]

The problem is there is significant uncertainty. This comes from the uncertainty in the projections of fertility, mortality, and migration. Also, the further we project into the future, the greater the uncertainty. To reduce uncertainty, the 2019 projection went only to the year 2100. Also, they used confidence limits instead of a range. Even this is only an effort to quantify the uncertainty. In the end, some things like population projections are difficult to know with much certainty far into the future.

COLLAPSE

Beyond all this, there is another mechanism that can affect populations. It comes from the discipline of ecology and is the idea of carrying capacity. Ecological systems can only support a limited population over the long term. Populations can grow above that, but they degrade the habitat that supports them. This can lead the population to collapse to a lower level. This phenomenon is common and well documented in animal populations. Applying this idea to humans usually brings up a set of comments like these: Yes, but humans are smarter and can use technology to increase the carrying capacity. Or, yes, but humans can see the system is being degraded and can change their ways. These are logical retorts, but the evidence supporting them is mixed at best.

In his book *Collapse*,[30] Jared Diamond chronicles several isolated, historical societies that faced resource depletion due to over-population. There were some that were able to avoid collapse and some that were not. For examples of societies that collapsed, think of Easter Island. It seems this population over-used resources. Over time the island could no longer support the population. Another example is the great Mayan civilization in Central America. It appears changing climate caused the collapse. Both of these societies appeared to be thriving until suddenly they weren't.

Human civilization has become so large and powerful that we can affect the entire planet. The clearest example of this is climate change. Since we can affect the entire planet and have nowhere else to go, we are an isolated society. We are much like Jared Diamond's historical societies, so we have about even chances of avoiding collapse. Some isolated societies have been able to avoid collapse. Iceland survived in a harsh environment for over 1,100 years.

There is also the story of three Pacific islands. Small Tikopia with only 1.8 square miles was sustainable for 3,000 years. For medium-sized Mangaia with twenty-seven square miles, deforestation caused it to collapse. Tonga with 288 square miles survived for 3,200 years. Analysis of these islands showed a bottom-up approach worked in small Tikopia. Here everyone could be familiar with each other and the entire island. A top-down approach worked in Tonga. It was large enough to develop an effective central government. Medium-sized Mangaia was too large for a bottom-up approach. It was also too small to de-velop an effective central government. Ironically, the earth's human population may be too large for either a bottom-up approach or a top-down approach.

Safa Motesharrei, Jorge Rivas, and Eugenia Kalnay modeled this behavior. Their model explains what happens to populations as they exceed environ-mental capacity. It is a simple but powerful dynamic model, yet it exhibits the types of collapses and stabilization observed in history. Their paper, *Human and nature dynamics (HANDY)*[31] is available online. Their abstract is clear and succinct in summarizing their work. I show it below:

> "There are widespread concerns that current trends in resource-use are unsustainable, but the possibilities of over-shoot/collapse remain controversial. Collapses have occurred

frequently in history, often followed by centuries of economic, intellectual, and population decline. Many different natural and social phenomena have been invoked to explain specific collapses, but a general explanation remains elusive.

In this paper, we build a human population dynamics model by adding accumulated wealth and economic inequality to a predator-prey model of humans and nature. The model structure, and simulated scenarios that offer significant implications are explained. Four equations describe the evolution of Elites, Commoners, Nature, and Wealth. The model shows economic stratification or ecological strain can independently lead to collapse, in agreement with the historical record.

The measure "Carrying Capacity" is developed, and its estimation is shown to be a practical means for early detection of a collapse. Mechanisms leading to two types of collapses are discussed. The new dynamics of this model can also reproduce the irreversible collapses found in history. Collapse can be avoided, and population can reach a steady state at maximum carrying capacity if the rate of depletion of nature is reduced to a sustainable level and if resources are distributed equitably."

The simple model can show economic inequality or environment limits can lead to collapse. This is a sign they may have captured some important mechanisms. Their model also shows by changing a few parameters it can achieve equilibrium. With different parameters, it can be with or without overshoot. Overshoot occurs when a population exceeds environmental limits. It then comes down to a lower equilibrium or collapses. This is common in animal populations. It can also happen in isolated human populations like Easter Island. It is important to note economic inequality can also cause collapse by itself. This is another reason to solve climate change and economic inequality together. I implemented HANDY in an Excel spreadsheet (Handy.xlsx). It is downloadable from my website in case you would like to play with it.[32]

So where do we stand? We are too large for a bottom-up approach. We are large enough to develop an effective central government, but for us that means a global government. The chances of developing an effective global government in time to solve the climate crisis are vanishingly small. Still, there are rays of hope. More than 2,500 cities[33] have made pledges to fight climate change. In 2015, 181 (of 196) members signed the United Nations Framework Convention on Climate Change. This Paris Agreement[34] has the goal of keeping the global temperature rise to not more than 2° C, but it would appear it is not strong enough to achieve this goal, yet if we can face our problems and make wise decisions, perhaps we can beat the odds.

SLOWING GROWTH

The population is an important factor used to project the size of the global economy. The size of the economy is an indicator of resource use. The uncertainty around population projections and the possibility of collapse can be unnerving, but just because we don't know everything doesn't mean we don't know anything. We know the current world economy is large enough to affect global systems. We also know the population is likely to continue growing even if at a slower rate. We know much of the world's population lives at a subsistence level and would like to live better. This puts more demands on resources. We must do more to slow population growth.

There are things we can and should do to slow population growth. One thing that can have a significant effect is to provide family planning education. Another is to make contraceptives readily available to anyone who wants them. These have a dramatic effect on countries with high fertility rates. Another effort along these lines is to educate girls and empower women. This is particularly effective in developing countries. More educated and empowered women often choose smaller families. Such actions to slow growth will increase the urgency of the economic reforms I will discuss in Chapter Nine but should improve our chances of avoiding the worst effects of climate change.

AGE DISTRIBUTION

The U.N. work also projects the distribution of the population by age. This shows populations are aging in most countries. This makes intuitive sense; as fewer babies are born, there are fewer young people, and as people live longer, there are more old people. This causes a problem. As the population ages, there are fewer working-aged people (often fifteen to sixty-four years old). There are more dependent people (children who are zero to fourteen years old and the elderly who are sixty-five years old or older). This is often measured by the dependency ratio. That is the number of dependent people divided by the total number of working age people. The global dependency ratio is expected to rise from 52.5% in 2010 to 65.7% in 2090.[35] The rise is more dramatic in every region but Africa where it is expected to fall from 81.2% in 2010 to 55.7% in 2090. Today Africa has many children compared to working-aged people. As the fertility rate drops, fewer children are born. A large number of today's children move into the working age group. Together, these reduce the dependency ratio.

The increasing global dependency ratio makes it harder to support the dependent population. Combining this with lower economic growth, governments can't afford to support the dependents. Most likely government debt will increase. Debt is the subject of the next chapter.

CHAPTER FIVE

DEBT AND OTHER CONSTRAINTS

The problems of climate change, economic inequality, and financial stability are interrelated. They have many aspects that we must address at the same time. In this chapter, I will discuss a few of these aspects. This includes debt, economic stability, and campaign finance. I also discuss why GDP is not a good indicator of progress.

DEBT

Governments can respond to the increasing cost of dependents in three ways. Either they amass more debt, reduce benefits in some way, or increase taxes. Government debt in many countries is already at historically high levels, leaving little room for further increases. Excessive debt can cause economic crises. Reducing benefits seems inescapable. People are living longer and healthier lives. Increasing the retirement age at which benefits start is a logical approach, but this is a reduced benefit, which is very politically difficult, as the elderly often are active voters. Their increasing number will further increase their political power.

Few politicians are willing to bet their jobs to do what is right. They will need to find some political cover. In some ways, this seems like an unsolvable quagmire. It may be possible to reduce benefits for the few wealthy retired people while fully supporting the rest. I will discuss that more in Chapter Eleven. In the past, high economic growth could provide more tax revenues to help reduce debt, but with slower economic growth, this will not work.

It is most likely there will have to be some combination of benefit reduction and tax increase. Before I can have the discussion about debt, I need to spend some time on money. You may be asking why I need to talk about money. Herman Daly said, "Anyone who thinks they understand money has probably not thought about it enough."[36] When most people think about money, they think about currency, that is, coins and bills. In modern economies, most money is lent into existence by banks. This is because our system of banking employs fractional reserves. This means banks are only required to keep a small fraction of deposits and are free to lend out the rest.

In the U.S., the Federal Reserve is the central bank. The Fed, as it is known, requires most banks to maintain a minimum reserve of 10% of net transaction accounts. Net transaction accounts are basically deposits. Small banks have lower requirements.[37] So for every $1,000 deposited, $900 can be lent to someone else. The borrower is free to put that money in their bank, thereby creating $900. The borrower's bank is then free to lend out 90% of the $900, and the process continues.

For a 10% reserve requirement, banks can create a maximum of 10 times the initial deposit. Our initial $1,000 deposit from above can create $10,000. Of course, most people don't borrow money to put in the bank. They borrow money so they can use it. They may put it in the bank for a while and then spend it. The person to whom they pay the money they borrowed may also put it in a bank at least for a while, and so it goes. If bank managers think bad times are ahead, they may elect to keep a larger reserve. The actual amount of money created is therefore less than the maximum. As economies grow and need more money, it is lent into existence, a process that also creates more debt.

Over time we have built a mountain of debt. Excess debt causes most of the severe economic recessions like the great recession of 2008 and 2009. Also, recoveries from debt recessions tend to be long and weak. Determining how much debt is too much is very difficult. It is difficult to recognize when the economy is in a debt bubble and even harder to accept.

Allowing banks to lend money into existence gives away to the banks the sovereign right of governments to issue money. An alternative system is for the government to issue money itself. This has seldom ended well, as the urge to print money to pay for government activities is overwhelming. Over time, this leads to runaway inflation.

Another option is for the central bank to raise the reserve requirements and buy government bonds. In some countries, including the U.S., the European Union, and Japan, the central banks did exactly this in the great recession of 2008 and 2009. This was necessary to provide market liquidity and fiscal stimulus. Market liquidity is the ability of a company or individual to buy or sell assets without undue effect on their price.[38] Fiscal stimulus is increasing government spending without increasing taxes.[39]

During good economic times, increased government spending is usually funded by issuing (selling) government bonds. However, in the great recession, central banks purchased government bonds. This created money with a few strokes of computer keys. It increased market liquidity and funded fiscal stimulus. In the U.S. the Fed decided to take that money out of the system over time. They did this by letting the federal government pay when the bonds mature. I will discuss a version of this option to reduce debt and manage the money supply in Chapter Ten.

INSTABILITY

Recessions are a built-in part of our economic system. Recessions are generally defined as two consecutive quarters of contracting GDP. Economists divide the year into four three-month quarters. When the GDP goes down in a quarter, it is contracting. Excess debt causes some recessions as discussed above. High-interest rates can also cause recessions. The central bank often raises interest rates to fight inflation. Higher interest rates usually cause increased household saving rates and reduced investments by firms.

Government austerity policies can cause still other recessions. Governments often put in place austerity policies to reduce debt. Austerity policies cut government spending without reducing taxes. This reduces the size of the economy and may cause recessions. Financial stock or housing bubbles can cause recessions when they burst. Bubbles exist when the price of something goes much higher than what makes sense. Bubbles almost always burst, and then the price comes down fast. When they do, they cause recessions. Finally, international effects from trade and currency valuations cause recessions.

Understanding what drives economic recessions is far beyond the scope of this book. Economists have been trying to figure that out for centuries. They have had only partial success. Still, they have made some progress in reducing the severity of recessions and accelerating recoveries. An excellent book on this subject is *Business Cycle Economics* by Todd A. Knoop.[40]

Recessions are of interest because, with reduced growth, it takes a smaller reduction in the growth rate to trigger a recession. There are ways to make our economic system more robust. These include higher bank reserve requirements. This reclaims at least part of the sovereign right for the government to issue money. Also included are constraints on stock exchanges (like Wall Street) to limit speculation. I develop these and more in Chapter Ten.

CAMPAIGN FINANCE

The changes required to reform economic systems will constrain some of the privileges of the rich and powerful. These privileges include the ability of banks to lend money into existence. Another privilege is the ways for CEOs to manipulate stock prices to their benefit. They do this using stock buybacks and options. The rich and powerful will not give these privileges up without a fight. To make needed changes requires a stronger voice from the rest of us.

Our current campaign finance laws allow the rich and powerful to buy influence over our government. This didn't happen by accident. The rich and powerful have worked on it for decades. This culminated in the U.S. Supreme Court decision known as Citizens United. This decision allows some strange things into our laws. It says corporations are people too, money is free speech, and giving unlimited money to buy influence is not corruption. It has led to super PACs (Political Action Committees) financed by the rich and powerful. All this has led our elected officials to represent the rich and powerful and not the overall citizenry. Giving power back to the majority of the people requires campaign finance reform. This is discussed in Chapter Seven.

GROSS DOMESTIC PRODUCT

I spent a lot of time discussing how to project GDP and how we use it as a measure of progress. Now I will dig in a little deeper. GDP is the monetary value of all finished goods and services purchased. Economists limit it to be within a geographic area over a specified amount of time. This is often a country but can be a region, a city, or the whole world. It is generally calculated quarterly, but the yearly numbers are considered the most important. GDP can be nominal or real. Nominal GDP is expressed in current currency. Real GDP is adjusted for inflation by using a constant currency, for example, 2010 dollars.[41] We can add

GDPs from different countries to get a global GDP. We convert GDPs from different countries to the same currency before summing them. This conversion can use the exchange rate, but it is more often done using Purchasing Power Parity (PPP). PPP is another means of comparing currencies. It uses a conversion rate so a basket of goods costs the same in different countries.

All this is background information on GDP. So what goes into GDP, and is that a good measure of prosperity? It includes all purchased final goods and services. It includes the money spent to design and build the Deepwater Horizon drilling rig in the Gulf of Mexico. It also includes all the money spent cleaning up the mess that followed the oil spill from that rig. Things that are not purchased are not included, so household chores, raising children, and yard work we do ourselves is not included. Robert Kennedy eloquently described this in his 1968 speech at the University of Kansas as follows[42]:

> "...Gross National Product counts air pollution and cigarette advertising, and ambulances to clear our highways of carnage. It counts special locks for our doors and the jails for the people who break them. It counts the destruction of the redwood and the loss of our natural wonder in chaotic sprawl. It counts napalm and counts nuclear warheads and armored cars for the police to fight the riots in our cities. It counts Whitman's rifle and Speck's knife, and the television programs which glorify violence in order to sell toys to our children. Yet the gross national product does not allow for the health of our children, the quality of their education or the joy of their play. It does not include the beauty of our poetry or the strength of our marriages, the intelligence of our public debate or the integrity of our public officials. It measures neither our wit nor our courage, neither our wisdom nor our learning, neither our compassion nor our devotion to our country, it measures everything in short, except that which makes life worthwhile..."

Kennedy used the Gross National Product, which was the convention at the time. GNP includes income from abroad as well as within a geographic area. GDP includes only income generated within a geographic area. Otherwise,

Kennedy's perspective is still relevant today. GDP measures the size of the economy, not any other measure of progress. It is wrong to think of GDP growth as progress. Fortunately, better measures are available and are now often calculated.

There are two measures of progress I prefer. First is the United Nations Inequality-adjusted Human Development Index (IHDI).[43] The other is the Genuine Progress Indicator (GPI).[44] The IHDI includes life expectancy, education, and per person income. This is then adjusted for inequality. The GPI uses ecological economics as its basis. It includes twenty-six economic, social, and environmental indicators. GDP is still useful to measure the size of the economy. It is not a measure of progress, although it is commonly viewed as such. Progress should be measured by other indicators like the IHDI and the GPI. I will discuss these further in Chapter Eleven.

PART II:
SOLUTIONS

The solutions presented in Part II are not drop in solutions. Rather they are developing ideas that fit into a plan. They provide solutions to the issues discussed in Part I. While I cover them at a high level, many of them are being debated and developed by others. They are in various stages of completion. They will need to be further developed and debated by our legislators. Support for many of them is not high enough to demand action by our legislators to implement them, but support is significant and rising for most of them. Part II describes them in enough detail that you can make your own informed decisions. When discussion and debates arise, you can take part with confidence. You can also see how they fit together to better meet all our needs. This includes rich and poor, current and future citizens, and Americans and people from other nations.

CHAPTER SIX

WHAT DO WE REALLY WANT?

In Part I, I covered a lot of ground describing where we are today. I talked about climate change and why it seems so difficult to accept and act on. This led to exploring the relationship between energy use and GDP and how global GDP growth has been slowing for decades and is projected to continue. I looked at how inequality is getting worse in the U.S. and other countries and the insidious effects it has on our well-being.

The global population is projected to slow, but there are uncertainties. There is even a possibility of population collapse. To avoid this, we need to further encourage the slowing of population growth. We need to deal with the consequences of aging populations. I talked about the mountain of debt we are generating and economic instability. This led to a discussion of campaign finance reform and of GDP as a poor indicator of progress.

This is so much information that it is difficult to wrap our minds around it. There are so many issues that we get overwhelmed. The good news is these issues all have workable solutions. These lead to a world where we are all better able to live meaningful, enjoyable, and fulfilling lives. That's worth working toward.

Before I can get into the solutions, I need to define what we want. I can't begin to have any idea of what you want. I can only look to those who have tried to understand what people in general want. As discussed in the Introduction, we can use Maslow's hierarchy of needs; Physiological needs (food, water, shelter, sex, rest, etc.), Security and Safety, Belonging (intimate relationships, friends, and family), Esteem (accomplishment, recognition, prestige, etc.), Fulfillment (purpose, achieving full potential, happiness, etc.). There is ample criticism of Maslow's hierarchy of needs in the academic world, but somehow it resonates with people. When we see it, it seems to make intuitive sense to the average person.

In today's world, to meet basic needs, we need economic stability. We can't meet our needs to be safe or secure while worrying about losing our livelihood in the next recession. This could mean losing our ability to meet our physiological needs. We want to have some sense of fairness in our world. Children seem almost born wanting fairness. How many times have we heard children say, "But that's not fair"? I talked about how many adults feel they are not getting their fair share of a growing economy. Finally, we need a stable and healthy environment.

Humans have been fortunate to have a stable environment for the last few thousand years. The last ice age ended about 11,700 years ago. The Bronze Age began about 5,000 to 6,000 years ago. Since then, humans have made tremendous progress. This progress would not have been possible without a stable climate. Now we are putting that stability at risk. We are warming the planet by emitting CO_2 by burning fossil fuels and thus destabilizing the climate.

These do not cover all our wants and needs, but Maslow's hierarchy plus a sense of fairness, and a stable and healthy environment and economy will cover the needs and wants of most people. As I discussed in Part I, many of the rules we have chosen to define our economic system do not support these needs, but we do have the power to change the rules of our economic system. For clarity let's list some goals that will be needed to change those rules:

- Provide an effective response to the climate crisis.
- Provide a fair distribution of wealth and income.
- Stabilize the size of our economy and our population at a sustainable scale.
- Stabilize our financial system so we can thrive in a low or no growth economy.
- Use a valid indicator of progress while clarifying GDP only measures the size of the economy.
- Build and maintain an effective government.

The rest of Part II outlines a set of policies that will lead to a more stable and fair economy. They will also lead to a stable and healthy environment that allows people to flourish.

CHAPTER SEVEN

REDUCING POLITICAL INFLUENCE

CAMPAIGN FINANCE REFORM

Without campaign finance reform, it will be difficult or perhaps impossible to achieve the goals set forth in the last chapter. The interests of wealthy individuals and large corporations dominate our current government. As discussed earlier, this leads to a playing field that is too tilted in their favor. These wealthy individuals and large corporations like it that way. They will fight tooth and nail to maintain it and even tilt it more in their favor.

Unfortunately, money drives this fight. Wealthy individuals and large corporations are willing to spend huge amounts of money to gain influence over the government. This influence is more subtle than what is generally considered corruption. There is generally no obvious quid pro quo, literally something for something, but more generally it is a favor or advantage in exchange for something. There is no conversation that says something like, "I will give you this money, and you will do what I say." It is more like an unstated agreement that is something like, "I will donate to your campaign, but I expect you to look out for my interests," yet it is no less effective than outright corruption. Effective campaign finance reform can limit the power of money to buy influence. It can also encourage contributions from the many.

The problem of the few having power over the many has existed for more than 2,500 years. The term democracy first appeared in the Greek city-state of Athens in the 5 B.C. Power struggles existed long before that. As soon as groups of humans formed, some form of leadership developed. It was most likely based on fighting prowess or decided by a consensus of the group. Social animals like chimpanzees have power struggles as Jane Goodall learned as she studied them in Tanzania. She found they even have different leadership styles. She studied two dominant alpha male chimpanzees she called Freud and Frodo. Freud maintained power by forming alliances. Frodo maintained power by aggression and fighting prowess. The point of this short diversion is power struggles to rule have been going on for all human history. We are not going to end them with any campaign finance reform. All we can hope to do is level the playing field to achieve confidence and effectiveness in our government.

The meaning of democracy was and is rule by the people. There are three main forms of democracy. In a direct democracy, everyone votes on every issue. Representative democracy is where citizens elect officials to represent them. In a constitutional democracy, a constitution limits the majority and protects the minorities. In the United States, we have a representative democracy limited by a constitution. Other forms of government include aristocracy, oligarchy, and plutocracy. In an aristocracy, an elite group rules. In an oligarchy, a few individuals rule. A plutocracy is where the wealthy rule. Still, other forms of government have rule by a single individual. In a monarchy, royal status legitimizes the ruler's power. In a dictatorship, an individual seizes power.

To complicate matters, there are various versions and combinations of these types. A constitution may constrain the power of a monarch. An example of this is Great Britain. Democracy may be in name only. For example, in Russia elections are not free, and a few wealthy individuals hold power. There is a gray area between democracy and plutocracy. Even in the United States, democracy is not pure. Over the years, there have been many efforts to limit the voting rights of minorities. Think of slavery, poll taxes, gerrymandering, and strict voter identification rules. The wealthy have undue influence on the government. Think of Political Action Groups attack ads or even Russian meddling. Those who live in democracies must be constantly vigilant.

The need for campaign finance laws in the United States became clear in the 1828 Presidential election, won by Andrew Jackson. Wealthy individuals and corporations started contributing large amounts of money toward campaigns. Of course, they expected to get influence in return. The first attempts at campaign finance laws started in the late 1860s. It continued in fits and starts until Congress passed the Tillman Act of 1907. This act limited direct contributions to federal candidates, and corporations and national banks were prohibited from making them, but it had weak enforcement and was ineffective. Between 1907 and 1971 Congress made and passed several more attempts, but they were ineffective because of many loopholes and poor enforcement. In 1971 Congress passed the Federal Election Campaign Act. This act required disclosure of campaign contributions. In 1974 outrage over the Watergate scandal provided Congress with political cover. It passed amendments to the 1971 Act. These provided a system of campaign finance regulations. They also created the Federal Election Commission to enforce them. This was the first effective modern campaign finance law.[45]

Congress tried without success to strengthen campaign finance laws between 1974 and 2002. Finally, in 2002 Congress passed the Bipartisan Campaign Reform Act. This act eliminated all soft money and increased hard money limits. Soft money is a contribution to a party or committee while hard money is a contribution to a candidate.[46] There are two types of committees. First, there are Political Action Committees (PACs). The second is independent-expenditure-only political committees called Super Political Action Committees (Super PACs). Super PACs may accept unlimited contributions. The Campaign Reform Act also banned electioneering communications (broadcast ads favoring a specific candidate) funded by corporate or union contributions.

The law was soon challenged on constitutional grounds. From 2006 to 2010 there were several cases heard by the U.S. Supreme Court. The decisive one was Citizens United v. Federal Election Commission in 2010. This case struck down limitations on electioneering communications funded by corporations or unions on the grounds that limitations infringed upon First Amendment rights to free speech. I like to think of the Citizens United v. FEC case as "corporations are people too." This means corporations have all the rights citizens do.

Finally, in 2014 the U.S. Supreme Court heard the case of McCutcheon v. Federal Election Commission. That case confirmed the Citizens United v. FEC limitations were unconstitutional. They infringed on the First Amendment right to free speech. This is where we stand today. This unlimited money has exacerbated the division of Congress down party lines. Now it is almost completely dysfunctional. The wealthy individuals and large corporations are more than happy to let it stay that way. A dysfunctional government cannot pass laws, so it cannot restrict the ability of the wealthy to keep the playing field tilted in their favor. It can also not effectively enforce the laws it has. We are becoming the Wild West where anything goes. For wealthy individuals and large corporations, it's party time.

There are limited options available to implement campaign finance reform. It is unlikely that a future U.S. Supreme Court would reverse the Citizens United v. FEC or the McCutcheon v. Federal Election Commission decisions, and even if it did, it is not likely to happen within the time frame needed to address climate change.

The U.S. Constitution could be amended to limit campaign contributions, but constitutional amendments are difficult by design. A constitutional amendment requires a two-thirds majority of both the House of Representatives and the Senate. Finally, three-quarters of the states must ratify it. It is hard to imagine achieving this given the dysfunctional state of government. Also, it could not happen soon enough to tackle climate change.

There have been some innovative ideas concerning campaign finance laws. Some do not appear to infringe on First Amendment freedom of speech rights, but they limit the effectiveness of contributions from the wealthy and large corporations. In 2002, eight years before Citizens United v. FEC, Bruce Ackerman, and Ian Ayres, professors at Yale Law School, proposed a promising new approach. Their book, *Voting with Dollars: A New Paradigm for Campaign Finance*, describes their proposal.[47] It is a system in which each citizen gets a monetary voucher. It is only good to support political candidates. If candidates receive contributions from the vouchers, it limits money from conventional contributions. There is an exception to avoid any First Amendment freedom of speech infringements. Candidates can choose not to receive contributions from the vouchers. If they do, they would be free to raise as much money as they could. In the voting with dollars approach, each citizen could get a voucher. For example, it could be $50. Tax revenues would fund the vouchers. Candidates of the citizen's choice could receive money from the voucher. If everyone who votes contributed the $50, it would raise over $6 billion. This is comparable to the total funding generated by federal candidates.[48] Eliminating some subsidies could fund this system. Many subsidies go to wealthy individuals and large corporations. These subsidies total hundreds of billions of dollars. In Chapters Eight and Nine, I propose the elimination of many subsidies that are not beneficial.

A variation of this system would be to make contributions anonymous.[49] Making donations anonymous would eliminate using campaign donations to influence candidates because the candidates would not know where there donations originated. Bruce Ackerman and Ian Ayres argued for anonymous contributions in their 2002 book. All donations including vouchers and contributors own money would go to the Federal Election Commission (FEC). The FEC would aggregate the contributions. Then they would send the money to the designated candidates. Anyone could donate an unlimited amount of their own money to the candidates of their choice. This includes individuals, corporations, and unions, but it excludes foreign entities. The candidates could use the money as they wish. To make sure the donations stay anonymous, it would have to be illegal to reveal their origins. Penalties would include very large fines and jail time. This is the campaign finance reform I advocate. Congress lacks only the will to pass it.

What chance is there such a system might become law? At first glance, it seems like it is a pipe dream, but a couple of recent candidates have raised large amounts of money from many small donors. The first was Bernie Sanders in the 2016 Democratic presidential primary. He raised $228 million, almost 60% of which was from small donations that averaged $27 each.[50] In the 2018 Texas Senate race against incumbent Ted Cruz, Beto O'Rourke raised over $70 million, and almost half of it came from small donations.[51] The rest of the funding for these candidates came from wealthy individuals and a few companies. Almost none came from PACs. Sanders and O'Rourke did not win, but they came more or less from nowhere and came very close to winning. Many small donations can add up to significant funding, and they represent a lot of votes. The landscape could change quickly. Also, with anonymous funding, candidates would not have to sell their souls to get elected. A system like this could look very attractive to Republicans and Democrats alike.

In 2015 Seattle passed a voting with dollars voucher law for city elections. There were several studies to assess the effectiveness and the degree of success seemed to depend on who funded the study, but it seems clear the donors were more evenly distributed by age and income level.[52]

I am encouraged this could be the cusp of changing the funding of political campaigns. This could create a government that better represents the will of the people.

Each U.S. state has some representatives in the U.S. House of Representatives. The population of the state determines the number of representatives. The state government divides the state into districts. This happens every ten years after the national census. Voters within each district elect a representative. In some states, an independent commission defines the districts, but in most states, the political party in power divides the state to their advantage. This is gerrymandering. The term comes from a governor of Massachusetts named Elbridge Gerry. In 1812 he defined an odd-shaped district north of Boston to favor his political party. The district was shaped somewhat like a salamander, and it came to be called "Gerry's salamander." Over time this became "gerrymander," and the practice became known as gerrymandering.

Since then, there have been efforts to make laws that prohibit the practice, but it is difficult to tell when gerrymandering was used to make the districts in a state. Many states have laws that require some variety of compact districts, but it is difficult to define compact. Beyond that, compact districts do not have to be fair districts.

A November 2018 *Scientific American* article, Geometry v. Gerrymandering by Moon Duchin, discussed these issues.[53] It also proposed a mathematical tool to evaluate districting. As a simplified example to show the potential effect of gerrymandering, the article depicts a square area to be divided into ten districts. Say the square is ten miles on each side. The example divides the square into one hundred smaller squares, one mile on each side. The results of an imaginary election show that sixty of the one hundred smaller squares vote for one party and forty smaller squares vote for the other. The larger square is then broken into what the author considers to be ten fair districts. The results are that six districts vote for the dominant party and four for the other. This matches the percentage of the larger square.

There are two tactics used in gerrymandering. First, there is packing. This crams similar voters into a few districts, making it difficult for their votes to count in other districts. The other tactic is cracking, which spreads likely voters of the opposing party across many districts, thus diluting their power. Some combination of the two tactics is also used. By using these tactics on the example cited above, the authors created two more district plans. One resulted in a ten to zero split favoring the dominant party. The other resulted in a four to six split favoring the non-dominant party. It is easy to see neither of the two plans would allow a fair representation of the will of the voters. This shows the power of gerrymandering.

To determine if a plan is fair, Moon Duchin proposes comparing the outcomes of all the possible district plans. Unfortunately, for real-world problems, the number of possible district plans becomes too large. Fortunately, mathematicians have developed a way to test a representative sample of all the possible district plans and then use that sample to assess fairness. So far the courts have upheld this approach, and I am hopeful redistricting after the 2020 census will use it.

CLOSE THE REVOLVING DOOR

The term "revolving door" describes the movement of personnel between government and business. Sometimes it involves positions that regulate business and the businesses they regulate. When this happens, it facilitates influence. When people move from being a regulator to a company they regulated, they bring two things. First, there is the knowledge of the process of making regulations. The other is connections to the people making the decisions. This allows companies to influence regulations. When they move in the opposite direction, they bring knowledge of how business works. They also bring a tendency to advocate for their former companies or industries. In either case, they provide companies with political influence. In the first case, they work for a company and facilitate influence. In the second case, they work for and influence the government regulators and hope to profit when they return to business. In either case, they are well compensated for this work.

Congress has attempted to limit this influence by requiring various waiting periods before regulators can move to industries they regulated. It is most often one to three years. The idea is that time reduces the value of relationships, but these efforts have not been effective. For example, the aids of legislators are not allowed to lobby their former bosses for a year, but there is a caveat. There is a salary limit below, which there is an exemption. Aids reportedly ensure their salary stays below the limit, so they can lobby right away.

All this influence peddling erodes public confidence in our government. In 2013, Transparency International conducted a poll that showed that 64% of Americans felt, "a few big interests looking out for themselves" ran the government.[54]

This is a sad state of affairs, but it is also a threat to democracy, which depends on public trust and confidence.

Sometimes the revolving door loop contains a third point. For example, an individual may start out as a congressional aide, move to a regulated company, then become a lobbyist on K Street (a figure of speech for the lobbying industry). It got the name from K Street in Washington D.C. where many lobbying firms are located.

So do lobbyists provide a useful service? Or are they instruments of wealthy individuals and large companies to exert influence? The answer is both; they provide Congress with expertise Congress itself doesn't have. Lobbyists often write draft legislation, but that comes with a cost. Their input tilts the playing field in favor of their clients.

Lobbyists also raise money for representatives' and senators' election campaigns. Given our campaign finance laws, this is a very useful service to congressmen. It makes them more likely to accept the lobbyist's draft legislation. This does not only occur in Washington, D. C. but also in state legislatures. In state legislatures resources to write legislation are even scarcer.

The financial resources needed to write legislation have been cut in various efforts to reduce government costs, but this is penny wise and pound foolish. The American people still pay to have their laws developed and maintained. Only now they pay in the form of excess corporate profits, some of which fund lobbyists, so the American people pay to have laws written. The difference is legislation written by lobbyists will be geared to their client's interest, not the American people's interest. It is a small wonder 64% of Americans think we have a rigged system.

There is a solution to the revolving door and lobbying influence problem. It is to provide financial resources for our elected officials to develop their own, in-house competencies for drafting legislation. This would allow them to better develop, analyze, and write legislation that best serves the majority of the people.

CHAPTER EIGHT

TWO DEGREES CELSIUS

"We basically have three choices: mitigation, adaptation, and suffering. We're going to do some of each. The question is what the mix is going to be. The more mitigation we do, the less adaptation will be required and the less suffering there will be."

John Holdren, President Obama's science adviser
and Director of the Office of Science
and Technology Policy on climate change.

To avoid the worst consequences of climate change, we must reduce the emissions of greenhouse gases. Climatologists agree we must limit the global average temperature increase to 2° Celsius above pre-industrial times. If we don't, there will be severe consequences. In December 2015, the United Nations Framework Convention on Climate Change reached the Paris Agreement. This addresses greenhouse–gas emissions mitigation, adaptation, and finance.[55] One hundred eighty-one countries have agreed to it. The U.S. has announced its intention to get out of the agreement, but the earliest it can is in November 2020. The agreement is far from perfect. The goal of the agreement is to keep the temperature increase to well below 2° C. It also has the long-term temperature goal to hold global average temperature increase to "well below 2°C above preindustrial levels and pursuing efforts to limit the temperature increase to 1.5°C above pre-industrial levels."[130]

The 1.5°C stretch goal was added to address the needs of the most vulnerable countries. The agreement is a bit strange in that it allows each country to set its own voluntary CO_2 emissions reduction goals. If you add them all up it is not enough to limit the increase to 2° C let alone 1.5° C, but that may be the only way to get 181 countries to agree to anything. This agreement is only a start; to be successful, it needs more aggressive goals with mandatory commitments. I am optimistic over time we will succeed, but it is far from certain, and the road will be very bumpy indeed.

CARBON TAX

The best way to reduce greenhouse gas emissions is to put a price on the emission of CO_2. This can be in the form of a tax or a cap and trade system. Other greenhouse gases are treated as CO_2 equivalents. For simplicity, I use the term CO_2 to include all greenhouse gases as equivalent CO_2 emissions. Either a tax or a cap and trade system can work if done well, yet it seems a tax would be easier to negotiate and put in place. In either case, we need a price for CO_2 that provides sufficient incentives to reduce emissions to a target level. This price (tax) will start at a low level to avoid shocking the economic system. We need to start this as soon as possible. It will increase to a maximum in about the year 2050 to accelerate the reduction of CO_2 emissions. After that, it can slowly be lowered over the next couple of centuries as technologies mature.

Integrated assessment models provide a tool to optimize CO_2 prices. They can estimate the CO_2 prices that meet a certain goal. For example, a goal could be a minimum increase in global surface temperature. Another is to maximize the discounted total utility of consumption over some period. Utility is an economic term for the satisfaction a person gets from consuming a product or service. A dollar value for utility can be determined by what people are willing to pay for the product or service. Total utility in this context is the utility all the people in the world get from all the products and services they consume. Discounting is a means to include the fact that future benefits are valued less than current benefits. Would you rather receive one hundred dollars today or a year from now? Finally, the goal could be to do both by maximizing the discounted total utility of consumption subject to a temperature increase constraint. I will discuss this below.

I used a modified Dynamic Integrated Climate-Economy (DICE)[56] model to calculate target prices for CO_2 in future years. DICE is a simple but powerful model developed by Dr. William Nordhaus at Yale University in 2012. Dr. Nordhaus has made the model available online in the form of an Excel spreadsheet.

As the name implies, the DICE model has a climate model integrated with an economic model. The climate model is a simple global model of atmosphere, land, and shallow and deep ocean temperatures. It calculates heat flow among the four. It also includes temperature forcing based on the amount of CO_2 in the atmosphere. CO_2 emissions depend on the GDP and the energy intensity of the economy. The climate model matches more sophisticated climate models well.

The economic portion of the model employs a simple growth model like I discussed in Chapter Two. It includes a damage function that reduces GDP based on the atmospheric temperature increase. The model optimizes a global price for CO_2 emissions by maximizing the discounted utility of consumption. The model runs over the years 2010 to 2305 in five-year time steps. Artificial end effects contaminate the last few decades, so the interesting behavior happens by 2250.

Once I had a model I understood and could change, I found there were a few areas that needed improvement. First, I added a model of renewable energy that explicitly accounts for the capital required for the transition from fossil fuels. This depends on the projected cost of photovoltaic cells. This is the cost when installing at a utility scale. More production reduces this cost. A higher price on CO_2 emissions encourages more photovoltaic cell production. This smooths the beginning of the transition of CO_2 price implementation. It also shows we can indeed afford the transition.

Second, I used a modified damage function that shows a greater penalty for business as usual. Damage functions account for economic output lost due to the effects of increased temperature. They are often a percentage reduction. The damage may take several forms. It could be from more severe weather, hurricanes, and floods. It could also be more severe droughts and wildfires. Lastly, it could take the form of rising sea level and ocean acidification.

The damage function in DICE is a simple function of increased temperature squared. This function has a solid foundation based on a compilation of estimates by various studies, but all the estimates lie within the temperature increase range of 1 to 3° C. This is fine when the temperature increase is below 2°, but the temperature increase for the base case of business as usual is almost 7° C. In the range of temperature increases from 3 to 6° C there are several tipping points. Any of these could significantly increase the severity of the damage. Uncertainty is very high in this range. All this is best discussed in *The Climate Casino*.[57]

Another damage function developed by Rezai and Ploeg[58] is available. This function matches the DICE damage function very well up to about a 2.5° C change in temperature. After that, the severity increases much faster. It follows work by Weitzman[59] and Ackerman.[60] It assumes the fraction of output lost due to increased temperature is 50% at a 6° C increase and 99% at 12.5° C increase. The uncertainty is so high above a 3° C increase, it is impossible to tell which function may be more appropriate, yet Rezai seems to better represent the very different world we would experience with very high increases in temperature. This is the damage function I adopted. When used in the integrated assessment model, it makes the business as usual case look much worse. That makes it clearer our best path forward is to deal with climate change aggressively.

Third, the growth model used in DICE results in a level of economic growth too high to be consistent with historical data. It uses a simple Solow model like Equation 2.1. It uses an exponential curve for the total factor productivity projection that increases at an increasing rate. As I show in the Appendix, a logistic curve is a better approach to fit the total factor productivity. However, I chose a simple linear curve to project the total factor productivity because I wanted to maintain the DICE model as much as possible. The most interesting time frame for addressing climate change is the next fifty to seventy-five years. Over that time frame, there is not too much difference between the logistic and linear curves. In the future, it may make sense to use the Solow model shown to Equation A.1. This includes a logistic curve to project the total factor productivity.

Finally, I added the ability to limit the temperature increase. The latest version of DICE includes this feature, but the version I worked with did not. It is a simple addition, but it does make the optimization a bit trickier. In any case, it is necessary to make any relevant policy recommendations, since most proposed goals include a maximum temperature increase.

With this modified DICE model I was able to optimize the price of carbon emissions over time. This maximized the discounted utility of consumption subject to a temperature increase limit. I first analyzed the case where the increased temperature limit was 2° C. The first case assumes we had a serious global action plan implemented in 2015. We could stay below a 2° C temperature increase by applying an approximately linear increase in the price of carbon emissions. This would start at $2/ton in 2015 and increase to $289/ton (in 2015 dollars) in 2045 and then decrease over time. It is sometimes useful to think of carbon emission pricing in dollars per gallon of gasoline. These numbers would then be $0.02/gallon in 2015 and $2.59/gallon in 2045. The model assumes the business as usual price of carbon emissions is $1/ton or $.01/gallon.

Suppose we get a serious global action plan implemented in 2020. Then the numbers change to $0.04/gallon of gasoline in 2020 and $2.59/gallon of gasoline in 2045. After the peak, all the prices follow the same path down. This is because there is a backstop price of other technologies that goes down with time. If we get a serious global action plan implemented in 2025, the numbers change to $0.09/gallon in 2025 and $2.59/gallon in 2045. The longer we wait, the less time we have and the higher the initial price needs to be. The options starting as late as 2035 are in Table 7.1 below. Also, each option shows the year in which the temperature increase equals 2° C.

Year	Start Year				
	2015	2020	2025	2030	2035
2015	0.02	N/A	N/A	N/A	N/A
2020	0.08	0.04	N/A	N/A	N/A
2025	0.23	0.18	0.09	N/A	N/A
2030	0.42	0.48	0.46	0.26	N/A
2035	0.61	0.68	0.81	1.04	1.00
2040	0.89	0.97	1.13	1.49	2.33
2045	2.59	2.59	2.59	2.59	2.59
2050	2.53	2.53	2.53	2.53	2.53
2055	2.47	2.47	2.47	2.47	2.47
Year at 2° C	2110	2110	2105	2105	2105

Table 7.1. Carbon emission prices in $/gal gasoline for various start years with a 2°C limit.

If we wait until 2040 to get a serious global action plan implemented, it is too late. We will not be able to limit the temperature increase to 2° C by pricing carbon emissions alone. It would take some other drastic action. This could be rationing gasoline or banning coal-fired power plants. I am not advocating such actions. I am advocating a sense of urgency to act now.

I did a similar exercise with a 1.5° C temperature increase. As you might expect, we have even less time to act. How much less time surprised me. The analysis shows in 2015 it was already too late to limit the temperature increase to 1.5° C by pricing carbon emissions alone. It requires drastic actions as described above.

What are you to make of this? First, you need to remember these are projections, not predictions. There is considerable uncertainty in both the climate model and especially the economic model. Still, there is enough here to say we have only a small window of opportunity to act against climate change. The best climatologists in the world think a 2° C increase in temperature from preindustrial times is the most we can allow. More than that risks crossing tipping points such as those mentioned in Chapter One. Passing these tipping points will change how the climate works. Most likely this will be in ways that make human life on anything like our current scale impossible. What's worse is these changes may be irreversible on anything like the timescale of human lives.

Carbon dioxide takes centuries to cycle out of the atmosphere. If the tipping points are triggered, the atmospheric temperature will continue to rise for a long time even if we completely stop CO_2 emissions at some point. This is because the oceans are currently absorbing most of the heat that is being trapped in the atmosphere. The huge mass of the oceans responds only over long time periods. This is pretty bad in anybody's book. Sure there is uncertainty, but our best understanding is the consequences are severe and long-lasting. Again, we have only a small window of opportunity in which to act.

In the face of uncertainty, what are we to do? If we do nothing and our understanding is correct, then the results are catastrophic. What happens if we act against climate change and our understanding is wrong? Then we spent a lot of resources to convert our energy system to emit less CO_2 for a little better climate. Because the economy links to climate change, we also spent significant effort to make our economic system more stable and fair in low growth conditions. As I have shown, these low growth conditions are already starting in any case. Over the long term, we will have to transition our current energy system to a renewable one.

There are various projections of how long we will be able to power our transportation system on oil. These are in the thirty to fifty-year range. Projections for the coal supply are longer. They are in the range of one hundred to two hundred years. If we could burn all that without destroying the climate, we might have enough for thirty to two hundred years. This would mean our understanding of the climate is completely wrong. That is extremely unlikely.

Our choice is to do nothing and risk catastrophe or spend resources now on things we may have been able to delay for a few decades. Perhaps an example that is familiar to most of us would help clarify our situation. If we buy homeowner's or renter's insurance, we pay money every year for something we hope we will never need. We lose the money we pay for insurance. We buy it because we can't afford to have our home and/or all our stuff destroyed by a calamity, say a fire. In case of a fire, we would still lose our stuff, but we would be financially compensated so we could rebuild and restock our homes. Even if we are among the lucky few who could afford to rebuild and restock our homes without insurance, it is not worth the risk. I view acting on climate change as buying insurance.

The analogy is not perfect. In the case of insurance, we lose our money, but the money we pay for a CO_2 emission tax is not lost to us. It can be designed to be revenue neutral. For instance, the government could return it to citizens as part of a basic income. Besides, we get economic benefits from acting on climate change.

Over time, the money saved by spending less to repair the damage caused by climate change will exceed the amount paid in taxes. It is as if the people of society are making an investment in themselves and their children. The effort to make our economic system more stable and fair is something we need to do as well. We will end up with a more stable and fair economic system and a more stable climate and save money. To me this sounds like a win-win-win situation.

Let's work together toward an increasing global tax on CO_2 emissions by the year 2025. In the first year, the tax would be about \$10/ton of CO_2 emissions (\$0.09/gal gasoline). This would increase to \$289/ ton of CO_2 emissions (\$2.59/gal gasoline) in 2045, and then reduce over time. The price would be adjusted to account for inflation.

FOSSIL FUEL SUBSIDIES

Fossil fuels include oil, gas, and coal. These form from the decay of the remains of living organisms over millions of years. A fossil fuel subsidy is any government action that tilts the playing field in favor of fossil fuels. It is usually something that will lower the cost of fossil fuel production. Lowering production costs includes direct funding and tax benefits, but most of it is a range of more subtle advantages. For example, a government could provide access to land or water at below market prices, or it could reduce the cost of capital by reducing the interest rates on loans. This is often done using loan guarantees, or it could fund research and development to benefit the fossil fuel industry. The government may also keep prices artificially low, which encourages using more fossil fuels.

The global scale of such subsidies is mind-boggling. Global estimates are in the range of $775 billion to $1 trillion per year.[61] It is difficult to estimate the true amount because many of the subsidies are subtle. Also, estimates may need information that is difficult to get. For example, consider a price control used to lower the cost of energy to the consumer. To estimate its value, one would need to know what the price would have been without the intervention, or suppose the government is providing resources at below market value. To estimate their value, we need to know the market value. Like estimating most things, this results in uncertainty. In any case, the numbers are huge. These estimates do not include the damage caused by climate change. Nor does it include the costs of the adverse health effects due to burning these fuels, and they do not include the massive military expenses or the lives lost while protecting the flow of oil.

This is often the practice of developing or oil exporting countries. That is where the biggest subsidies lie, but those are not the only countries to use them. The estimate for subsidies in the United States is about twenty billion dollars. The top ten countries in order starting with the highest subsidies are China, Iran, Saudi Arabia, Russia, Venezuela, Indonesia, India, Egypt, Algeria, and Mexico.

These subsidies act as a negative price on carbon emissions. This is the exact opposite of what I advocated above. They provide incentives to find, develop, and use new sources of fossil fuels. These are new sources we cannot burn if we are to stay below a 2° C temperature increase. The capital investments encouraged are long-lasting. These investments fund oil refineries, coal-fired power plants, and pipelines, which lock in the continued use of fossil fuels for a long time.

The good news is these subsidies have decreased in recent years. Economists don't like subsidies because they are inefficient and cause distortions. Their opposition against fossil fuel subsidies has been consistent. China is the current leader of the G20. It is also the biggest offender, yet it has committed to working with the G20 nations to reduce fossil fuel subsidies. The G20 is an international organization with rotating leadership. It includes nineteen countries plus the European Union. Together they represent about 85% of the global GDP. They also represent about two-thirds of the global population.[62] I am hopeful the G20 will make significant progress, but talking about something and actually doing it are quite different. Still, there is some reason to be cautiously optimistic.

CHAPTER NINE

FAIR DISTRIBUTION

I have discussed how we are able to make choices that lead to better outcomes. In the last chapter, I discussed a policy choice of taxing CO_2 emissions to stabilize our climate. I will explore policy choices to improve the stability of the economic system in the next chapter, and I will address how to actually get these choices implemented in Part III. In this chapter, I will discuss several policy choices designed to achieve a fairer economic system. These choices are mostly in the spirit of leveling the playing field.

One obvious way to level the playing field is to collect more tax money from those who can most afford to pay and use that money to fund programs discussed in this chapter to reduce inequality. Highly progressive inheritance and income taxes have been used successfully in the past and could be reinstated. These and other ideas are the focus of this chapter.

INHERITANCE TAXES

As of 2016, the United States estate tax exemption amount is $5.45 million (it increased temporarily to $11.4 million for 2019 to 2025) and the maximum rate is 40%.[64] So only 0.2% of estates pay any tax. The estate tax could be structured so there is no effect on, say, 90% of the people. Then for the top 10%, the marginal tax rate could increase linearly (or similar steps) from 18 to 77%. With today's estate value distribution, this results in any estate under $2.5 million not being taxed, and the top rate would apply to estates with values greater than $14 million. Could the U.S. ever pass such a law? From about 1940 to 1980, the U.S. had a similar law (see ninety years and counting[65]). In 1977 for example, the exemption was $120,000 and the maximum rate was achieved at $5 million. In today's dollars, that is about $460,000 and $16.4 million, respectively.

From about 1980 to the present, the tax has been gradually reduced to end up in today's estate tax law. How did that happen? For decades, the richest Americans have been systematically influencing politicians to reduce taxes including estate taxes. They funded political campaigns, think tanks, and universities to advance their agenda. They convinced the 99% their interests are the same as that of the 1% (see *Dark Money* by Jane Mayer [66]). What are our chances of enacting a highly progressive estate tax?

As long as unlimited money can be used to usurp our political system, there is practically no chance. This type of tax has been given the unfortunate derogatory moniker of "death tax." I think a better name would be the "fairness tax." Our way out starts with campaign finance reform, (see Campaign Finance Reform [45]). We need to let our political representatives know campaign finance reform and a highly progressive estate tax leading to a more equal society is in everyone's best interest. Only then can we breathe life back into the American Dream and pave the way for a post-growth society.[63]

To summarize, as of 2016, the United States estate tax exemption amount was $5.45 million (it temporarily increased to $11.4 million in 2019) and the maximum rate was 40%.[64] In 1977 the estate tax exemption amount was $460,000 in today's dollars, and the maximum rate was 70%. Revenue collected from the very wealthiest people could be used to fund policies to improve economic mobility such as improving primary education and making college more affordable. Economic mobility is the ability of an individual or family to change their economic status.[67] This is usually measured by a change in economic status from one generation to the next.

Many people in the United States pride themselves on our equality of opportunity. We believe this sets us apart from other countries, yet the data does not support this. The U.S. has the second lowest economic/social mobility among developed countries. Only lower is the United Kingdom in a close race. This means, in the U.S., if you are born rich or poor, you are more likely to stay that way than if you were born in, say, Denmark. This is evidence of a tilted playing field that favors the rich.

Children born into rich families have many advantages over those born into poor families. It starts with more access to quality prenatal and pediatric health care. Then there is access to adequate nutrition and a more interesting and varied environment. Then there is high-quality preschool education. The children of rich families are much better prepared when they enter the school system. The school system they enter is of higher quality. They achieve this by attending a private school, or their parents can choose to live in a school district with higher quality schools. When leaving high school, more of them go to college. The colleges they attend are more often prestigious. This may be due to legacy benefits or direct donations to the college. Legacy benefits are a preferential treatment to the children of alumni. They leave college with no student loans to pay. Having a prestigious college on their resume helps them get the best jobs.

The advantages don't end there. Throughout their lifetimes, each of their parents can give each child up to $15,000 (2018) per year, so the total is $30,000 per child per year. There are no taxes on these gifts.[68] Also, there is a lifetime exclusion of $11.2 million. This means parents can give up to an additional $11.2 million to the children tax-free.[68] For example, if you give a child $50,000, then $15,000 is covered by the yearly exclusion and $35,000 contributes to the lifetime exclusion. When the parents die, there is another $5.45 million estate exemption ($11.4 million through 2025). All this money goes to the children without a penny of tax paid by either the parents or the children. No wonder children of rich parents are likely to stay that way.

In addition to more progressive estate tax rules, the gift tax laws would also need updating. At least the $11.2 million lifetime exemption would need to go. After all the exemptions, the giver pays a gift tax at a rate of 18% to 40%. These rates would change to match the inheritance tax rates. I know wealthy people feel it is their money and they already paid income tax on it. They feel there should be no more taxes on it, yet if the HANDY model is correct, we must deal with inequality to avoid population collapse. The HANDY model is uncertain. So dealing with inequality is at least an insurance policy against population collapse. Wealthy parents can still have the annual exemption of $15,000 per parent per child and the proposed $2.5 million estate tax exemption. How many advantages do children of rich parents need? They would still have all the advantages of their upbringing.

PROGRESSIVE INCOME TAX

Progressive income tax has a long history in the United States dating back to 1862. At that time, a progressive income tax helped fund the civil war. Progressive income taxes tax higher levels of income at higher rates. Over the years from 1862 to 1872, the tax rates varied from 3% to 5% in 1862 to 5% to 10% in 1866. After that, they went down to 2.5% by 1872. All these income taxes had an exemption. Income below that amount was not taxed. The Revenue Act of 1870 let the income tax law expire. From 1873 to 1893, there was no income tax. In 1894 an income tax law passed, but the Supreme Court declared it unconstitutional in 1895. After that, there were no income taxes until 1913.

The Sixteenth Amendment to the Constitution allowed Congress to tax all income. During World War I the maximum tax rate went up, but the high rates were only applied to very high incomes. The maximum rate came down to 25% in 1925 and stayed there until 1932. Then a large increase passed. In retrospect, that was not the wisest fiscal policy during the depression. Economic understanding at the time could offer no better guidance. Tax rates stayed high through the depression and skyrocketed to a maximum of 94% in 1945 because of World War II. After that rates stayed very high until the early 1960s when Congress reduced the maximum rate to 70%. Since the early 1980s, it stayed between 35% and 40%, with a few exceptions. It has stayed there ever since.[90, 91] Wikipedia provides a nice graph that summarizes this history from 1913 to 2010.[90, 92]

There were a few decades of relative equity after World War II. This lulled the countervailing force to sleep. In the 1980s, wealthy individuals started their attack on income tax. After this success, they broadened their attack. They attacked our system of government. Then wealthy individuals joined with large corporations. Together they changed the rules of our economy. This tilted the playing field further in their favor.

In the 1950s most federal tax revenues came from income tax. Small amounts of payroll taxes and tariffs supplemented federal revenue. The 1980s saw lower income tax revenue and higher payroll taxes. The federal tax revenue was about the same. It was in the 15% to 20% range of GDP. Payroll taxes are regressive. That is, they tax lower income levels at higher rates. The 1990s saw a little lower income taxes and much lower tariffs as a percentage of GDP. Payroll taxes fill the void. As a result, federal taxes are much less progressive than they were in the decades after World War II. Often they are actually regressive.

Also, income tax laws have become too complex. They include many loopholes, exemptions, and deductions. Most people can't benefit from these, but wealthy individuals can hire an army of accountants and lawyers. They are able to manipulate their finances to reduce their tax burden. This is all legal of course because they wrote the rules.

The solution is to simplify the tax law so everyone pays their fair share. We should match the degree of income tax progressiveness of the 1950s and 1960s. This is a tall order under the best of conditions. It is among the most important changes, but it is the most contentious and difficult to achieve. The countervailing force must recover its former strength to achieve it.

UNIVERSAL BASIC INCOME

The idea of a universal basic income has been around for a long time.[69] One of the early advocates was Thomas Paine, the author of Common Sense (1775–1776). In an essay called "Agrarian Justice," he proposed giving a lump sum to every American when they turned twenty-one. A land inheritance tax would fund it, and it would serve as a basic income.

Our current welfare system is a convoluted tangle of programs and tests for inclusion. A universal basic income would replace much of our existing welfare system. It is not some utopian aspiration. A 2017 poll conducted by Northwestern University and Gallup found 48% of Americans support it. It is a way to give every citizen a share of the economic pie generated by the country. The idea is a monthly sum would go to all citizens who are at least eighteen years old. It would be enough to provide essentials on which to live. Of course, there would be an income tax on the basic income like any other income. This is a big idea. It would have to be implemented with care and over time.

A universal basic income is only one way to assure every American citizen can meet their basic needs. There seem to be as many different versions of support systems as there are countries. One of the attractions of the universal basic income is its simplicity. Our current system is a nightmare to administer and is full of perverse incentives. For example, consider the person who is on welfare who finds a low paying job in which he earns a little more than welfare provides, but it causes him to lose the welfare benefit. He would only net a small part of his pay. Losing his welfare is like having his income taxed at almost 100%. Why bother?

I wish I had a clear recommendation on how to put in place a universal basic income, but it seems the details have not yet developed. There have been and continue to be experiments in various places to work out the details, yet no consensus has emerged. The best we can do is encourage debate and experimentation to figure it out. It is an idea whose time is almost here.

Our current system of support tries to meet the goal of assuring basic needs. It has met with limited success. In 2017, my wife and I vacationed in the Pacific Northwest. We had never spent much time there. It is a magnificent part of America with a beautiful coastline, vibrant cities, and spectacular mountains. We also included a brief excursion to Vancouver and Victoria Canada. Besides the usual tourist attractions, a couple of things struck me that are relevant to this discussion.

We visited in the fall. Wildfires were still raging in much of the area. The fires closed the scenic drive along the Columbia River Gorge. Roads near Crater Lake and Mount Rainier were also closed, but we were able to see those spectacular sights. One morning when we were staying near Mount Rainier, we left our hotel to find our car (and everything else) covered with a thin layer of ash. It was only a minor inconvenience, but it was a clear reminder, because of climate change, our world was becoming a very different place.

More relevant to this discussion was the amount of homelessness in Portland and especially Seattle. Homeless people seemed to be everywhere in Seattle. They were even in the shadow of the Amazon headquarters. This was a stark contrast to our experience in Vancouver and Victoria where, over a few days, we saw a grand total of one homeless person. Victoria is a beautiful small city, so one could say it is easier to manage in a small city, but Seattle is only about 15% more populous than Vancouver. The difference was palpable. I'm not sure how Canada is handling homelessness better, but it is clear they are. We can do much better. Others already have.

MINIMUM WAGE

The United States has had a federal minimum wage since 1938. It started at $4.78 per hour in 2018 dollars. It reached its maximum in 1968 when it was $11.65 per hour in 2018 dollars. Over the years, it has increased many times only to see inflation erode it between increases. The last increase occurred in

2009 when it was increased to $7.25 per hour. It has been there ever since. It is currently $7.25 per hour in 2019 dollars. Besides the federal minimum wage, most states have minimum wages that are higher than the federal minimum wage. Fourteen states match the federal minimum wage while two are lower (Georgia and Wyoming at $5.00 per hour). The states that are higher than the federal minimum wage range from just above it to $11.50 per hour in Washington.

Beyond federal and state laws, many cities have created their own minimum wages.[84] City minimum wages are generally higher than state law. They range up to a little over $15 per hour. Sometimes they also add caveats, like higher wages for city employees or lower wages for small businesses, or they add a minimum amount for health care or they are adjusted for inflation.[85] Employers pay the highest of the federal, state, and city requirements for their location.

Why do we have this hodgepodge of laws? Part of it is because the economic benefit is contested. Standard economic theory says a minimum wage reduces employment. It reduces employment particularly among the least skilled. Most economists agree with that because colleges and universities teach it that way, but economists who have studied the issue in depth come to a different conclusion. The majority of the evidence suggests there is no loss of jobs for moderate increases. It is not clear how much of an increase is moderate, which is another reason for debate.

Another reason for the hodgepodge of minimum wage laws is the cost of living varies across the country. New York City has the highest cost of living. Athens, GA has among the lowest. For every dollar spent in New York City, the residents of Athens, GA need only spend $0.60 to get the same things. Small towns and rural residents pay even less, so it makes sense to have a federal minimum wage level supplemented by higher state and city wage levels.

There have been many proposals for increasing the federal minimum wage. Senator Bernie Sanders has been pushing for a federal minimum wage of $15 per hour for some time. He has been pressuring Amazon to increase their minimum wage. Recently they have complied, but their reasons are not known. Amazon is a huge for-profit business. They must perceive some advantage beyond altruism in making the change. They will most likely now pressure their competitors to join them. In any case, it is a small step toward higher minimum wages.

What does an effective minimum wage law landscape look like? Robert B. Reich in his book, *Saving Capitalism*, advocates a federal minimum wage of one half of the U.S. median wage indexed to inflation. Is one half of the median wage a reasonable choice? There are two pieces of data that suggest it is. First, in the United States, in the 1960s the ratio of the minimum wage to median wage averaged 51%. Over the years of 1960 to 1979 it averaged 48%. Second, the average minimum wage of the 34 OECD countries over the years of 1960 to 2012 is 48% of the median wage. In 2018 the median U.S. wage was about $20 per hour; the current $7.25 per hour gives a ratio of minimum to the median wage of about 36%. Half of the median wage is about $10 per hour or well below Senator Sanders' $15 per hour. This approach does not address the wide variation in wages or costs of living throughout the US.

The Brookings Institute, a well-regarded think tank in Washington, D.C., studied minimum wage policies. They recommend state and city minimum wages that are half of the local median wage indexed to inflation. They also recommend a moderate federal minimum wage indexed to inflation.[86] They don't give guidance on what is moderate. One approach might be to adjust the 2009 minimum wage for inflation since then. That would result in a federal minimum wage of $8.32 per hour in 2018 indexed to inflation. This would be close to one half the local median wages in the state with the lowest wages. Mississippi and Arkansas tied for the lowest median wages.

Other states should pass their own minimum wage laws at one half their local median wages. Massachusetts would have the highest at $12.95 per hour in 2018. So the state minimum wage laws would range from $8.32 to $12.95 per hour in 2018. Cities could have their own minimum wage laws where they differ too much from the state average. Washington, D.C. has the highest median wage. Its minimum wage would be $14.05 in 2018 indexed to inflation. Some cities already have minimum wage laws with higher levels. A few small cities in California are already at $15 per hour. Los Angeles plans to get to $15 per hour in 2020.

This strikes me as a balanced, sensible approach, and one which I advocate.

CHIEF EXECUTIVE OFFICER PAY

Chief Executive Officer (CEO) compensation has skyrocketed in recent decades. In 1965, average CEO compensation was twenty times that of the company's average worker. Over the years, it has increased more and more. In 2018 average CEO compensation was 361 times that of the company's average worker. This is from a *Scientific American* article called "A Rigged Economy."[89]

This was an article written by Nobel Laureate economist Joseph E. Stiglitz. For large companies and financial institutions, CEO pay is often in the tens of millions of dollars, and it is not only the CEOs. Executives on the next level down also received excessive compensation packages.

CEO compensation had been rising in the 1970s, but it started to rise more rapidly in the 1980s and took off starting in the 1990s. As I have discussed several times, the market or economic system relies on a system of rules to exist. There were a series of changes to those rules that accelerated the rise in CEO compensation.

Executives and other high-level employees often receive stock options besides their salary. This gives an executive an option to buy company stock at a given price over a specified period of time. The price is often the current price of the stock or a discounted price. The specified period is often delayed for a few years. Sometimes executives may be able to buy a fraction of the stock in each of several years. Companies use this arrangement for a few reasons. First, it encourages employees to stay with the company without spending cash. It also makes employees feel like owners of the company. This is all well and good. Problems can arise when executives use inside information. It gives undue advantage used to time the buying and selling of their stock.

For example, companies sometimes buy back some of their own stock. This raises the price of the stock. This is because after the buyback there are fewer shares. The value of the company is not affected, so each share is worth more. Top executives are aware of the timing of the company buyback. They can buy their stock a little before the company buyback and sell a little after for a profit. This type of insider trading was illegal until 1991, but it was difficult to prove and not well enforced.

From 1932 until 1982, companies were not allowed to buy back more than 15% of their shares of stock. This limited the value of this type of insider trading but did not eliminate it. In 1982, under President Ronald Reagan, the SEC removed this restriction. The SEC is the Securities Exchange Commission. This cracked the flood gates. In 1991, the SEC allowed executives to sell their stock options without public disclosure. This made this type of insider trading legal. Finally, in 1993 President Bill Clinton signed a bill that allowed companies to deduct executive compensation. This reduced the corporate income tax. Companies only deduct compensation over one million dollars if it depended on performance. This allowed companies to compensate executives and reduce taxes. Executive pay in the form of stock options increased, as did company stock buybacks. This opened the flood gates completely.

Both political parties helped remove these restrictions. It doesn't matter which party is in power. The influence of wealthy individuals and large corporations is omnipresent.

The solution is straightforward, but like many of these reforms, it will most likely be difficult. Robert Reich provides a path forward in *Saving Capitalism*. He would define fraud to prohibit all forms of insider trading. Any use of corporate buybacks by CEOs to raise share prices and cash in on stock options would be illegal. This was the case before 1991. The timing and extent of corporate buybacks must be disclosed. This was the rule before 1982. Any stock trade based on insider information would also be illegal. It is straightforward but difficult to put in place.

SUBSIDIES

In the last chapter, we discussed fossil fuel subsidies and how they were hindering our response to climate change. Here we should note they are also tilting the playing field in favor of the rich. In this section, we will discuss a few other subsidies. I will start with agricultural subsidies. Like all subsidies, economists don't like agricultural subsidies. This is because they are inefficient, and they cause distortions.

Subsidies are generally created to encourage some group to do something that is good for the country they might not otherwise do. For example, it might be to produce more of a certain crop to feed the country or to produce less of a certain crop to support prices or produce more fossil fuels to help the country have enough energy. Some subsidies are outright handouts encouraging no clear action. For example, paying interest to banks on money they must keep in reserve by law. I will discuss this more below, but besides being inefficient and causing distortions, subsidies almost always tilt the playing field in favor of the rich. Why is that so?

It is next to impossible to foresee the future and provide the right amount of incentive. This means there are usually long debates. These create fertile ground for lobbyists of special interests to mold the law in their favor. Once a subsidy is in place, special interests fight tooth and nail to keep it or expand it. Politics make it very difficult to end a subsidy, and we have one more handout in our laws.

Many countries feel it is imperative they be able to feed their own people. Agricultural subsidies are seen as a way to do that, but they tend to have unintended consequences. Jokes abound about paying farmers not to plant things. Governments claim they are helping family farms, but big corporate farms and suppliers of farming equipment and chemicals dominate agriculture. Most subsidies end up in large corporate hands one way or another. In the end, these subsidies are more likely to be counterproductive than helpful.

The scale of agricultural subsidies is about one-half of fossil fuel subsidies. Agricultural subsidies amount to about $486 billion per year globally. Most of these subsidies are in Asia. China has $165 billion, Japan $65 billion, Indonesia $28 billion and South Korea $20 billion. The European Union has subsidies of over $50 billion, and North America is at $45 billion ($30 billion for the U.S.).[70]

These subsidies are in a few forms. The first is a direct payment to farmers. These are often intended to help poor farmers, but because of the structure of the agricultural industry, they often end up making rich farmers richer. Another form is crop insurance at below-market prices. The same arguments are often made against crop insurance. The final form of agricultural subsidies is price supports. These keep prices high to encourage farmers to grow certain crops. They usually take the form of tariffs or quotas to limit cheaper imports. They often result in overproduction of subsidized crops. They also result in higher consumer prices than necessary. There is much talk to reduce or end agricultural subsidies, but there does not appear to be much progress.

Government support for the pharmaceutical industry is even more difficult to estimate. The advantages they get are much more subtle and ingrained in the very fabric of the rules that define our economic system. They spend more on lobbying in the U.S. than any another industry. It is 42% more than the second place and related insurance industry. All this money and effort has allowed them to define the rules of our economic system that affect them. They have limited the power of the U.S. Food and Drug Administration to only check if a drug is safe. It may not check if it is effective or cost prohibitive.

By contrast, other countries have a review board that checks all three (safety, effectiveness, and cost). Australia requires new products provide enough evidence of safety, effectiveness, and cost. It must show the drug is safe, it is much better than what is available, and it is worth the cost. These systems are not perfect. People are only human. They must sift through mountains of information from the drug companies. Some of the scientific studies may be cherry-picked. Enough money will get you a convincing presentation on anything. Still the results tell the story.

The U.S. pays more for prescription drugs than any other country. For example, take Humira. This is an injectable medication used to treat rheumatoid arthritis and psoriasis. Patients in the U.S. pay more than three times the cost in Switzerland. Or Avastin, which treats cancer costs more than twice as much in the U.S. as Switzerland. The U.S. cost is over seven times the cost in the United Kingdom. Or Harvoni, used to cure hepatitis C, costs twice as much in the U.S. as Switzerland.[71] You get the point. Whatever other countries are doing, the rules that define their economic system are less tilted toward the drug companies.

The rules affecting the pharmaceutical industry in the U.S. result in a very effective subsidy for drug companies. Subsidies are often funded by governments through taxation of the public. Money from the majority is taken by taxation. It is then given to the rich minority through some industry. The drug companies have taken out the middle man (the government), so the money moves straight to them. They don't have to share the profits from their lobbying effort with the government. It has the added benefit that the amount of the subsidy is impossible to even estimate. The full extent of their advantages remains hidden.

There is another area where the pharmaceutical industry has influenced the government. It is advertising prescription drugs. Before the 1980s, drug companies thought their customers for prescription drugs were doctors. In 1981 Merck placed the first print ad for prescription drugs aimed at consumers. In 1983, Boots Pharmaceuticals aired the first television ad for a prescription drug. Before long, the government told them to stop. This started a long fight between the drug companies and the government. In 1985 the FDA agreed drug companies could advertise prescription drugs, but it required they disclose side effects and other information. The drug companies' continued legal battles focused on the First Amendment.

In 1997 the FDA loosened its rules. The drug companies had won. The U.S. is only one of two countries that allow such advertising. The American Medical Association has now taken up the fight. They want to ban direct-to-customer prescription drug advertising. It will be an uphill battle.[72] The countervailing force can help them. What else can we do to rein in drug prices? A simple first step might be to allow Medicare to negotiate Part D drug prices as the Veterans Administration and Medicaid do.

Another controversial subsidy is the Export-Import Bank (EXIM). Its goal is to increase U.S. exports. This bank operates as a company fully owned by the American government. It makes loans that are too big or risky for commercial banks. It is controversial first because it makes some loans to foreign entities. It is also controversial because there have been accusations of corruption. There appear to be at least conflicts of interest. As subsidies go, it is pretty small: about $2 billion per year. EXIM claims it generates billions in exports. Others say it loses money because of inadequate risk accounting. In any case, it is another example of a subsidy that favors the rich.

Banks receive many advantages from the government. Like the pharmaceutical industry, their subsidies are subtly built into the rules of our economic system. The most obvious is the bailouts in 2008 and 2009. Most people think that was a $700 billion bailout, but a report from Forbes in 2015 says the total commitment of government is $16.8 trillion. Of that, $4.6 trillion was already paid out.[73] Yes, those are trillions with a "T." We all know much of the bailout money went to pay huge bonuses to the very people who caused the problem.

That same Forbes article shows how the banks got the rules rewritten in their favor. It started forty years ago. Over time, they tilted the playing field in their favor. This was all done in the name of deregulation. By 2000 the changes were complete, and it was a Katy bar the door banking free for all. Of course, in 2008 it all tumbled down. The free marketers from the banks suddenly became socialists. They went begging the government for help. The government had to oblige to prevent the collapse of the global financial system. To prevent a recurrence, Congress enacted new regulations. Now, ten years later, the banks must have a bit more capital, but not much else has changed. Banks that were too big to fail are even bigger. The banks are even surer if things go bad, the government will bail them out again. Chapter Ten is all about restoring stability to the global financial system. I have included this discussion here as an example of how the rules of our economic system have been rigged to distribute money to the rich.

Another example is interest the Fed pays on the reserve money that banks keep by law. On first glance that may seem to make sense. They put money in, so they should earn interest, but that money is there to provide support if a bank runs into trouble. Banks have proved many times they can and do get into trouble and expect support. That support is ample compensation for reserving part of their money. The Fed operated for almost one hundred years without paying interest on bank deposits.

In 2006 Congress passed the Financial Services Regulatory Relief Act of 2006. That required the Fed to pay interest on the required and excess reserves.[74] Once the Fed started paying interest, reserves skyrocketed from about $100 billion to $1.6 trillion. The interest rate started at a low 0.25% and payments were "only" a couple of billion dollars per year. Now interest rates are over 2% and interest paid is about $50 billion per year. All this goes to the bank's bottom lines as profit. None of this would happen if not for the 2006 law.

I could go on listing examples of direct and subtle subsidies. Those listed above show the rules that define our economic system are full of subsidies. They transfer money from the many to the rich few. So what do we do? Because most subsidies are laws, Congress must act to reform the laws and phase out subsidies. It is very difficult for an average individual to have much effect on Congress. Sadly, representatives and senators pay almost no attention to individual letters. To get their attention, there must be huge numbers of them on a subject. There are non-governmental organizations (NGO's) that advocate phasing out subsidies. There are also some other resources. These are below.

- For fossil fuels, a good one is the Natural Resources Defense Council.[75]
- For agriculture, a good one is the National Sustainable Agriculture Coalition.[76] Search for subsidies.
- For pharmaceuticals, American Action Forum. Wikipedia is a good place to start.[77, 78]
- For the Export-Import Bank, the American Action Forum is also a good choice for export-import credit reform.[79, 80]
- Banking reform article in the Washington Post.[81]

I encourage you to get involved. Find one or two issues you feel strongly about. Start advocating for reform; sign petitions, and write letters. This means to write letters on paper and send them through the mail, not email, and, yes, support them with donations. Many small donations provide the resources to energize the countervailing power.

PATENTS

Intellectual property is the area of law that deals with patents, copyrights, trademarks, and trade secrets. I am going to focus on patents. A patent is a license given by a government authority to an individual or company that has a novel idea and reduces it to practice. Reducing it to practice means it must show the idea can produce something. It gives its owner certain exclusive rights. These include the exclusive rights of making, using, and selling a product for some period of time. This means no one else can make or sell a product covered by the patent without the patent owner's approval. If the owner elects to give approval, there is generally some monetary compensation.

The reason governments issue patents is to provide an incentive for innovation. They also help pay for research and development necessary to reduce the idea to practice. Patents create monopolies. The monopoly applies only to the product covered by the patent for a limited time. Like all monopolies, the patent owner can charge much more than the cost of the product. Only the availability of viable substitutes limits the amount charged.

The pharmaceutical industry charges outrageous prices for patented drugs. After the patent expires, generic drugs cause the price to plummet. Pharmaceutical companies are masters of maximizing the profit they make on patented drugs. The rest of us pay the price. Other industries can only aspire to pharmaceutical companies' patent skills. Generally, patents are in effect for a limited time, but slight modifications made to the product covered by a patent can themselves provide patent protection. This can extend the patent protections more or less forever.

In the United States, the term of a patent is twenty years from the earliest filing date and cannot be extended. For some products that change often, like computers or cell phones, that is more than enough. They are only novel for a few years, but for other products, like drugs, they will be novel for a long time until something better comes along.

So how do we change patent laws to maintain the incentive to innovate without providing windfall profits to patent owners? Unfortunately, there seems to be no consensus and limited research in this area. Still, there are a couple of common sense ideas that may make sense as a starting point. These are below.

1. Reduce the term of patents to ten years.
2. End the ability to extend the effective term of patents by modification.

Even these simple changes will be fiercely opposed by industry. Only by using the countervailing power of the many can we hope our elected officials will work to make patent law less tilted toward industry.

ANTITRUST LAWS

In recent times, antitrust laws only protect the consumer from monopolistic pricing. Even that is not used often to break up companies. This is because of the overwhelming power of large corporations. Only a few big break-ups come to mind, like AT&T in 1984 and Standard Oil way back in 1911, yet when antitrust laws started in the late 1800's, congress had something else in mind. One of its main goals was preventing concentrations of economic power. They did this to prevent economic power from becoming excessive political power. Remember, this was America's Gilded Age.

The Gilded Age is the name given to about the last quarter of the 19th century in America.[82] It corresponded roughly to the latter part of the Victorian era in Britain. It occurred in the early part of the Belle Époque in France. It was a time of rapid economic growth and grand buildings. For example, the Vanderbilt's Biltmore Estate in Ashville, North Carolina and the Breakers in New Port, Rhode Island. This led to a large influx of immigrants to provide the needed labor. It was the time of larger than life business tycoon dynasties. They had names like Vanderbilt (shipping and railroads), Rockefeller (oil), Carnegie (steel), and Astor (fur trade), yet it was also a time of great inequality.

The best way to think about the Gilded Age is to remember it was only gilded at the top. The top 2% of households held 1/3 of the wealth and the top 10% held 3/4 of it. The bottom 40% had no wealth at all. This compares to today where the top 10% of American households owns 76% of the wealth. The next 40% owns 23% of the wealth and the bottom 50% owns only 1% of the wealth.[83]

In the late 1800s, there was great concern about the economic and political power that resulted from concentrated wealth. The public and Congress shared this concern. Corruption was rampant and blatant. What we now think of as corporations were then called "trusts." In 1890, Congress passed the

Sherman Antitrust Act named after Senator John Sherman of Ohio. President Benjamin Harrison signed it into law in the same year. In its first years, the government used it against organized labor. This is almost the exact opposite of its intention. Power is never given up without a fight.

In 1901 President Theodore (Teddy) Roosevelt used the law to bring a lawsuit against the Northern Securities Company. Edward H. Harriman owned this company. It dominated transportation in the Pacific Northwest. Teddy talked about the lawsuit in his usual style. He said it "served notice on everybody that it was going to be the Government, and not the Harrimans, who governed these United States." He backed that up with lawsuits against DuPont and the American Tobacco Company. President William Howard Taft used the law to break up Standard Oil in 1911. Woodrow Wilson was President from 1913 to 1921. He also worried about the political power of concentrated wealth, but the time for bold action had passed.

After that, interest waned. The robber barons had been somewhat tamed. After the Great Depression of the 1930s and World War II in the 1940s, the countervailing force was well established. It made great progress on reducing inequality. This lasted a little over forty years. In the 1980s the pendulum started swinging the other way. One by one, constraints on business fell in the name of growth and the "free market." This was led by Ronald Regan in the U.S. and Margaret Thatcher in the U.K. Inequality started to get worse. The median income stagnated. The proceeds from economic growth were going to the top. This has continued through the 1990s right up to the present. Now our wealth distribution is back where it was in the late 1890s. It is once again time to strengthen the countervailing force.

Today it is not as clear who has too much political power, or whether breaking them up will solve the problem. Influence today is much more subtle than in the late 1800s. Companies no longer show up in a politician's office with bags of money. Their influence is more subtle and legal but no less corrupt.

It is more difficult to tell which companies to break up. For example, big pharmaceutical companies have exerted their political power to tilt the playing field in their favor, but developing drugs is very expensive. It is likely fewer new drugs would be developed if the big drug companies were broken into smaller ones. Except for banks, which I will discuss in Chapter Ten, there is no right answer about how big a company may be. Bigger companies enjoy the economy of scale, which in principle allows them to be more efficient and innovative. It can also allow them to use their political power to reinforce their position and squelch competition. This has the opposite effect of reducing efficiency and innovation. This is better handled with campaign finance and patent laws.

There are some industries that have consolidated to the point they are oligarchies. Consumers have limited choices. This is a clear case for breaking them up into more companies that can compete. Some examples are internet service providers and television channel providers. This includes cable and satellite TV companies. In many areas, there are only one or two choices, and we pay higher rates because of it. Another example is large hospital chains, which can limit competition in an area. In these cases, we need to enforce the laws we have.

A common tactic of wealthy individuals and large companies is to neuter laws they don't like. They do this by getting Congress to cut enforcement funding. Cutting enforcement funding is often easier than eliminating a law. It is about as effective. This tactic is not only used on antitrust laws. It is also used on any law wealthy individuals and large corporations don't like. We need to ensure there is enough funding to enforce the laws.

TRADE AGREEMENTS

Globalization has a dark side. It comes in many forms. The most common complaint is developing countries with lower wages, particularly China, are taking American jobs. China is a particular concern. There are safety concerns. There were toys contaminated with lead paint, unsafe baby food, and ineffective pharmaceuticals. There are concerns about competitive advantage due to inadequate environmental regulations. There are also concerns about the unethical acquisition of technology. This may be forcing companies to share their technology, or it may be a blatant disregard for patent protections. There have been accusations of dumping products on the world market at below cost. They do this to gain market share and to destroy their competition. Finally, state-sponsored enterprises in strategic industries are competing illegally. People in America and many other developed countries feel they are being taken advantage of on the world market. Part of this feeling comes from the fact the benefits of trade are not well distributed. In theory as well as in practice, there will be winners and losers in both countries. The hope is the winners will win more than the losers lose.

Still, global trade has exploded in the last twenty years. Countries have gone to great lengths to encourage it. What do they hope to gain? Economic theory says there are advantages to trading. Countries can have two types of advantages in trade. The first and easiest to understand is absolute advantage.[87] This is a situation where one country can produce something at a lower real cost than the other. The real cost is after exchange rates. If there is another product where the situation is the opposite, there are advantages to both countries to trade. Both countries win. Otherwise, there can be a third or fourth country involved completing the trading loop. They can all win. After a while, there is a complex trading network. If the exchange rate changes, so do the advantages. Other things like the relative interest rates between the countries affect the exchange rate.

The other type of advantage is comparative advantage.[88] Countries promote trade more often based on this idea. David Ricardo first developed the theory in 1817. In this case, say there are two countries that make two products. One country makes both products at a lower real cost than the other country. The theory of comparative advantage says both countries can still profit. Say France is much better at producing cheese than Portugal, and France is only a little better at producing wine. Both countries can profit. Say France produces enough cheese for both countries, and Portugal produces enough wine for both countries. When they trade, both countries win. This is difficult for most people to get their heads around, but it is true. It is true only if some assumptions are true. The terms of trade must be within a certain range. The terms of trade are how much each country charges the other for its product. There are a few other assumptions that must be true.

There are seven assumptions that are unrealistic in today's world. This calls comparative advantage into question. I will discuss a few of them. The first is capital and labor do not move between countries. In today's world, labor can move between countries. It may be slow, but it is significant. Even in Ricardo's time, labor moved to where it was scarce, for example, populating the United States. Today there are many examples of people immigrating to escape poverty or just to better themselves. This assumption by itself is enough to call comparative advantage into question. Another unrealistic assumption is production resources can move easily between industries. Economists generally consider production resources to be land, capital (buildings, equipment, etc.) and labor. It is very difficult to transform a steel mill into a computer chip factory, and it is difficult to retrain a steel mill worker to be an effective computer chip maker. A third unrealistic assumption is trade is always balanced. In today's world, trade is rarely balanced. These unrealistic assumptions are strong criticisms of comparative advantage. This calls into question the benefits of much of international trade.

The benefits of international trade are questionable. There are adverse consequences as discussed at the beginning of this section. There are two adverse consequences that are particularly relevant. These are environmental regulations and job losses. This is one of the most difficult areas in which we can make progress. Countries enter into trade negotiations hoping to achieve their own agendas. They hope to give as little as they can and gain as much as they can. Recent tariffs have been very low by historical standards, at least until President Trump's recent posturing. Modern trade deals are about other things. These include patent protection, environmental regulations, and regulatory barriers to trade.

Trade deals should not promote international trade at the expense of everything else. So what can we do on trade to help us solve the joint problems of climate change and economic inequality? First, we should push Congress to tax the carbon emissions embedded in imports. These should match our own carbon emissions taxes. When importing products, we get more than the products themselves. We get what is embedded in them. For example, when a desert country imports grain, it is also in effect importing water used to grow the grain. When we import steel, we are importing the carbon emissions that went into making that steel. Such a tax would encourage countries to reduce their carbon emissions, at least those embedded in the products they sell us. We can push our negotiators to include minimum wage requirements in trade deals. For all countries included in the trade deal, it should be at least half the median income of their lowest wage region. We should push for it to be half the median income in each region.

Beyond these conditions in trade agreements, there are things we can do at home. We should limit the burden trade imposes on the inevitable losers. We should use some of the gains from international trade to provide retraining. It should also provide financial support to affected individuals. It can supplement their income while retraining in a full-time educational program. It should maintain a high percentage of their pay. This should be for only a limited time, like a year or two. Robert Reich recommends 90% and 2 years. The process of defining who is eligible for this benefit is difficult and subject to abuse. We should avoid the difficulty and make it available to anyone who loses a full-time job.

CONCLUSION

The road to a fair economy is a long and torturous one. I have covered a long list of things to change. It took about seven decades for us to get to this situation. We will not fix it in a year or two, but it will likely take decades to complete. Still, I am optimistic we can awaken the countervailing force, and it is up to the task.

CHAPTER TEN

FINANCIAL STABILITY

The debate over business cycles has been going on for at least two centuries. Like other areas of economics, economists have made great progress, but their knowledge is quite incomplete. Exactly what causes business downturns is not known, nor is there a consensus on the best policy responses to minimize the damage. Despite our most heroic efforts to maintain economic growth, we still have recessions.

There are a few things we know about business cycles summarized from Todd A. Knoop's book, *Business Cycle Economics*.[40]

1. Aggregate demand and supply shocks are often causes of recessions. For example, say consumer confidence drops. When this happens, often demand for products and services drops as well. This is a demand shock. Economic growth slows or starts shrinking, and a recession occurs. An example of a supply shock might be a major war in the Middle East. The war causes a drastic reduction in oil exported from the region. Prices of gasoline go up, and people start to cut back, reducing economic output.

2. Imperfect labor markets can play an important role in business cycles. Wages are sticky. That means it is difficult to lower wages in response to slowing demand. People often quit their jobs rather than accept a wage cut. Unions may strike. Companies usually cut jobs

rather than wages. This increases unemployment and starts the spiral toward recession.

3. Imperfect information can lead people to cause recessions. If people expect a slowdown, they may save more and consume less, actually causing a slowdown. Even experts have imperfect information. The wrong policies can cause recessions as well.

4. Central banks try to keep a balance between unemployment and inflation. They do this by adjusting interest rates and using other tools. Our understanding is there is a natural rate of growth. This is the maximum rate of growth achievable without increasing inflation. It is very difficult to even estimate these rates, and they can change with time. If the Fed gets it wrong, it can cause a recession or high inflation.

5. There are three known things that can turn a recession into a depression. These are deflation, currency depreciation, and excess debt. An economic depression is a very severe recession that lasts longer and has slower recoveries. Deflation is a drop in overall prices. Currency depreciation is a devaluation of the currency compared to other currencies. Excess debt is debt that results in default.

6. Business cycles are getting more and more global. Countries can catch recessions from each other. This is because global trade and finances intertwine our economies.

Why are business cycles of interest to us? Recessions are painful. Some people lose their jobs and can't find new ones. Others also lose their homes and savings and even go into bankruptcy. These often take a long time to recover from, and some never do. This increases inequality. Another reason has to do with low economic growth. Global economic growth has been slowing for decades despite everything we can do to support it. There are good reasons to expect it to slow further whether we like it or not. When economic growth is already low, it takes only a small shock to cause a recession. Instead of war in the Middle East, a fire at a major oil refinery may be enough.

Finally, the world is awash in debt. Both government and private debt are at very high levels. Debt is not inherently bad. All debt is someone's asset or wealth. It is excess debt that risks making small recessions much worse. So when is debt excessive? Debt is excessive when the borrower can no longer service the debt. That means the borrower can no longer make payments on a debt and defaults.[93] When the borrower defaults, that portion of the lender's wealth is destroyed.

There are many things that can make debt that does not look excessive, suddenly become excessive. For example, say a homeowner has a mortgage with a fixed interest rate. The monthly payments are the same for the life of the mortgage. If the borrower loses his job and can't find another, he may no longer be able to make the payments. The bank will go through the necessary steps for foreclosing and take his house. Of course, the bank doesn't want the house and will try to sell it. Foreclosed houses generally sell for less than other, similar houses. This destroys some wealth. If this happens to many people in an area, the price of all homes goes down. Many homes may go underwater where the homeowner owes more than the value of the house. Many more homes will default. Significant wealth will be destroyed. People begin to spend less, and the recession deepens. This is like what happened in the Great Recession, which started in 2008.

As another example, say a company borrowed money for five years at a fixed interest rate with payments only covering the interest. The company pays the principal when the loan matures. Companies often rollover debt. This means when a loan reaches maturity, they take out another loan to pay off the principal. Over the five-year period, say interest rates increased. If the company cannot demonstrate it can make higher payments, it may not be able to get another loan. It would have to declare bankruptcy. This destroys wealth. The economy slows a bit, and a few more companies get in trouble and have to cut back. A recession starts and gets deeper.

If you are beginning to feel like our economic system is unstable, you would be correct. It is. Instability is where a small change can lead to large consequences. It is like walking along a mountain ridge where the mountain slopes steeply off on either side. I have walked such a path. It was a narrow path along a mountain ridge. The mountain sloped off steeply on either side. It was not so steep a misstep would cause me to fall to my death, but it was steep enough to make me uneasy. In some ways it was exhilarating. There was a beautiful view for miles off both sides. It was like being on top of the world, but when I was walking my eyes were on the path, not the view.

The choices we have made for the rules that define our economic system have left us in a similar situation. When things are going well, it can be exhilarating, but a small misstep can start a downward spiral. It is as if a group of people is walking along that mountain ridge tied together with a rope around their waists. One small misstep by anyone in the group could drag everyone off the edge. Governments and central banks try to correct when they sense the economy is slowing, but their knowledge is imperfect, and there are lags in the system. It takes time for them to notice, and their corrective measures take time to work. As economic growth slows, it gets harder and harder to keep everyone on the ridge. It is as if the path gets narrower and narrower. The smallest misstep is enough to send the group over the edge.

Our understanding of the business cycle is incomplete, yet there are things we can do to make our economic system more stable and more robust. I discuss these things in the rest of this chapter.

TOO BIG TO FAIL

The Great Recession started in 2008. It soon became clear some financial institutions were too big to fail. If any of these institutions were to fail, it was thought to be likely there would be a cascade of other failures with dire consequences. The economic system could freeze up and lead to a global depression. Faced with these "likely" consequences, the U.S. government had little choice but to bail out AIG. That was only the beginning. In the end, the bailouts included Fannie Mae and Freddy Mac, Citicorp, and Bank of America. Plus they propped up General Motors and Chrysler after they filed for bankruptcy. The full timeline is available online.[94] The total cost of the bailouts was over $1 trillion, though estimates vary. In any case, it was a huge amount of money. Much of that was in the form of loans, most of which were repaid, but not all.

What did these institutions do with this money? They used some to buy institutions that were in even worse shape. The government encouraged this. Somehow, at the time, it seemed to make sense. They also used some of the money to pay big bonuses totaling over $10 billion. These went to the very executives whose reckless behavior caused the problem. Most of those who lost their jobs and homes were not bailed out.

These institutions also received considerable scrutiny of their operations. This resulted in new regulatory requirements. These were intended to make the financial institutions less likely to fail. It is now ten years later. Some of the regulatory requirements have been relaxed. There is pressure for further relaxation. The financial institutions that were too big to fail are even bigger. This is in absolute terms and relative to the size of the economy. Financial institutions do have more reserves, but in short, we are no better off today and most likely worse.

While the bailouts were most likely necessary at the time, the actions taken to avoid repeating this disaster have been inadequate. The bailout reinforced the moral hazard. By moral hazard, I mean since these institutions know they will be bailed out, they can engage in more risky behavior. If successful, they reap the rewards. If their risky behavior goes bad, it threatens the viability of the financial system, and someone else pays. After the bailouts, institutions are even surer the government will have to bail them out again, encouraging more risky behavior.

The solution here is to target any company (financial institute or otherwise) that is too big to fail. They must be broken into smaller companies that can fail without collapsing the system. This should remove the moral hazard. It will be clear to companies if their risky behavior causes the company to fail, there will be no bailout.

Any company that is too big to fail is too big to exist. The focus here should be financial institutions. We must also check others like automotive manufacturers and tech companies. This includes oil companies like Exxon Mobil and Chevron. It also includes tech companies like Amazon, Google, Apple, Facebook, and Microsoft. These companies have too much market power. That leads to excess profits (economists call these rents). An article in *The Economist* estimates globally there are $660 billion of excess profits due to market power.[95] More than two-thirds of these are in the United States. The article recommends breaking large companies with excess market power into smaller companies. They recommend this to "rebuild public faith in markets, [and] restore competition". If the public faith in markets is rebuilt, perhaps confidence in government will also increase.

Existing antitrust laws focus on consumer protection against monopolistic pricing, but they also need to address the competitiveness of markets. Non-competitive markets lead to excess profits from market power. One-tenth of the U.S. GDP is in industries where four companies control two-thirds of the market. Corporate profits are at record levels. We need to strengthen antitrust regulators by supplying the resources they need.

GLASS-STEAGALL ACT

The Banking Act of 1933 is known as The Glass-Steagall Act.[96] It was a sweeping banking reform act with several provisions. It included the establishment of the Federal Deposit Insurance Corporation (FDIC). This protects depositors against bank failures, but I will be exploring a specific part of the legislation. It deals with the separation of commercial and investment banking.

Commercial banks are what most people think of as a bank. They accept deposits and then make loans to individuals and companies. They may also provide a variety of related services including checking accounts, credit cards, and debit cards.[97]

Investment banks are financial services companies. They do not accept deposits. They generally broker stock, bond, annuity, currency, commodity, and derivatives transactions. They also help companies with corporate finance. This includes issuing stocks and funding mergers and acquisitions.[98]

The Glass-Steagall Act achieved the separation of commercial and investment banks. Investment banks could no longer accept deposits. Commercial banks could not trade in securities, nor could they underwrite or distribute securities. The only exception was government securities. Finally, commercial banks could not share employees with companies that dealt with securities.

This system worked well for about thirty years. In the 1960s, federal banking regulators started to soften the Glass-Steagall Act. They allowed commercial banks to conduct some securities activities. This softening of the Glass-Steagall Act continued for the next thirty years. In 1998 the federal banking regulators allowed Citibank to join Salomon Smith Barney. Citibank was one of the largest commercial banks. Salomon Smith Barney was one of the largest security firms. The Glass-Steagall Act no longer separated investment and commercial banking. In 1999 Congress made it official and passed the Gramm–Leach-Bliley Act. This repealed provisions of the Glass-Steagall Act that prohibited commercial banks from affiliating with security companies.

Economists disagree on the impact these changes had on causing the financial crisis of 2007 and 2008. Joseph Stiglitz argued "[w]hen repeal of Glass-Steagall brought investment and commercial banks together, the investment-bank culture came out on top." That culture is one of freewheeling and risk-taking. This compares to the more staid culture of commercial banks. It is this risky behavior that led to the financial crisis. Ben Bernanke argued the causes of the financial crisis were not illegal. They were not even regulated by the Glass-Steagall Act. Bernanke is a former chairman of the Federal Reserve Board. It seems to me both Stiglitz and Bernanke were right. Risk-taking was not illegal or regulated by the Glass-Steagall Act, but putting investment and commercial banks together was now allowed by the new legislation. It created an atmosphere of risky behavior, which contributed to the crisis.

Requiring separate commercial and investment banking would be disruptive, but it would be a logical first step toward breaking up the too-big-to-fail banks. Excess risk-taking is destabilizing. Therefore, it should be discouraged. Some argue risk-taking drives dynamism, that is, vigorous activity and economic growth, yet global economic growth has been decreasing for decades. The cost of this risk-taking is too high. We are already exceeding environmental limits. Economic activity is emitting too much carbon dioxide and degrading our climate. We need to act to limit risk-taking, not further encourage it.

DAY TRADERS

Day traders speculate by buying and selling securities at a high frequency. This includes stocks and sometimes bonds. They do this to profit from small movements in price caused by some event. In the extreme, these people can buy and sell a stock on the same day. They believe by acting on some event before it becomes known by most people, they can profit from it. Some argue these people provide liquidity to the market. That means they provide a ready buyer when someone wants to sell a stock and vice versa, but the effect is what should be a minor event gets amplified. It is often turned into a major event in the stock market and sometimes beyond.

There is another type of rapid trading in stocks that also has a destabilizing effect. In automated trading, a computer algorithm controls the trades. These are computer programs owned by financial firms that watch many variables. They decide when to buy or sell a security. These programs connect to the stock exchanges. They can make trades in milliseconds. Companies choose to put their computers close to stock exchanges. They hope to gain and profit by making trades a few microseconds ahead of the competition. Other companies have similar computer programs with similar algorithms. When one program acts, it often triggers other programs to act, often cascading into a crash. This is crazy, I know, but they believe they can profit from these actions, and they most likely can.

There is a simple way to limit this kind of behavior. It is a transaction tax. Every time there is a security (stock, bond or commodity) transaction, it would be subject to a small tax. The tax could be a very small percentage in the range of 0.5% to 1% of the transaction. This should be implemented over time to avoid shocking the system. The proceeds from such a tax could be revenue neutral if the proceeds are returned to all adult citizens. It could be a part of a universal basic income.

THE FED'S ROLE

The Federal Reserve System has five key functions.[99]

1. Conduct the nation's monetary policy.
2. Help maintain the stability of the financial system.
3. Supervise and regulate financial institutions.
4. Foster the safety and efficiency of the payment settlement system.
5. Promote consumer protection and community development.

I will focus on the first three. These are very difficult functions. The results affect the well-being of almost all Americans and many globally.

Let's start with conducting the nation's monetary policy. Monetary policy manages the nation's money supply. The object of monetary policy is to manage the levels of unemployment and inflation. If the money supply is too large, it causes inflation over time. If it is too low, it drives up unemployment. To manage the money supply, the Fed has to know how much inflation or unemployment is too much. The Fed has chosen an inflation target of 2%. There seems to be a consensus that is a reasonable target. If inflation is too high, it reduces the real value of savings and wages. If inflation is negative (deflation), it increases the real value of debt. This can be destabilizing.

Unemployment is trickier. Economists think unemployment below a certain level increases inflation. The goal is for unemployment to be at that level, but that level is not known well. It can only be estimated. Beyond that, economists think it changes with time. Demographics, innovation, and cultural norms can cause it to change. Also, there are lags in the system. The Fed doesn't know all the parameters of the economy immediately. By the time the data is available and analyzed, it may be a few months old. When the Fed acts, the consequences of an action might not be clear for a year or more.

Finally, the money supply is not easy to adjust. The Fed can adjust the money supply by buying government bonds with money it created. This is quantitative easing. It has only used this in the Great Recession of 2008. The Fed's tool of choice to adjust the money supply is interest rates. It raises interest rates to reduce the money supply. It lowers interest rates to increase the money supply.

Managing the nation's money supply is like steering an ocean liner. Think of guiding the Titanic through a field of icebergs in the fog at night, only worse. You can only adjust speed by yelling directions to the engine room. You can't see very well, the engine room doesn't always get the message, and your ship takes a long time to respond to the rudder. Still, the Fed has done a reasonable job of keeping the economy out of trouble.

The next function is helping maintain the stability of the financial system. It is even more difficult. A narrow interpretation of this function is to maintain price stability. The Fed does by managing interest rates and the money supply as discussed above. The general interpretation of this function is to keep financial institutions from collapsing and causing a depression. Financial institutions can collapse due to excessive risk-taking. This is often in combination with a downturn that their risk helped to cause by creating an asset or debt bubble. When these bubbles burst, they can cause severe recessions with slow recoveries. The Great Recession of 2008 is a classic example of that. The Great Depression of the 1930s may have been the result of an asset bubble bursting in the stock market crash of 1929. Congress passed the Glass-Steagall Act in the wake of the 1929 stock market crash.

In September of 2008, the Lehman Brothers bankruptcy caused a crisis. It made it clear the wheels were coming off the economy. Over the next months and years, the Fed acted aggressively to stimulate the economy and provide liquidity. Liquidity is cash or other assets that are easily converted into cash. It did this by lowering interest rates to near zero. In normal times, this would encourage banks to make more loans. This creates money, which would provide liquidity, but in 2008, Lehman Brothers so frightened the banks that they didn't make more loans. The Fed decided to pump cash into the economy. It did this by buying government bonds with money it created (quantitative easing).

Besides the Fed action, the Federal government implemented expansionary fiscal policy. Expansionary fiscal policy is government spending more than revenues. It stimulates the economy. Together with the Fed action, this helped to avert a potential global economic catastrophe. The Fed is still unwinding quantitative easing. This means they are taking back the money lent to the federal government and destroying it.

Based on the way the Fed has acted since 2008, it believes keeping financial institutions from collapsing is part of its function, yet it was reactive. It did not take aggressive action until it was clear the economy was on the verge of collapse. There is a third, more general interpretation of helping maintain the stability of the financial system function. That is the Fed should use its authority to create rules that make the financial system more stable. This would include rules that make debt and asset bubbles less likely. It is pretty clear the Fed does not believe this type of action is part of its function, but if it did, what actions could it take? Before I get into how such a system might work, it would be helpful to take a brief detour to the history of fractional reserve banking.

Fractional reserve banking has a long history. It started out with goldsmiths who kept people's gold and other valuables safe for them. In return, they gave people a note for deposit. Soon these notes became tradeable, forming the first paper currency. After a while, the goldsmiths realized not everyone would want their gold at the same time, and they could lend part of it out for a profit. The goldsmiths became the first banks. This worked fine for a while, but when there were hard times, more people would come and demand their gold back. If too many people wanted their gold back, the goldsmith-banker could default. If people suspected many people wanted their gold back, there could be a run on the goldsmith-banker. In this case, everyone would try to get their gold back while there still was some gold to get. When this happened, the goldsmith-banker would default, and anyone who didn't get their gold out in time would lose it.

For a while, these bank runs were common. In 1668 Sweden established the first central bank. It could require a minimum reserve and act as a lender of last resort. This reduced bank runs but did not eliminate them. In the United States in 1933, the Glass-Steagall Act established the first deposit insurance. By 2014, 113 countries had established deposit insurance. About forty more are considering it. This made bank runs a thing of the past.

Fractional reserve banking has not been without its critics. These criticisms are in a few areas. The first area is the creation of money by lending. The main argument is the money multiplier discussed in Chapter Five doesn't depict how money is created. Rather, critics claim the demand for credit controls the money supply. The money multiplier approach is far from perfect, but it does give a basic idea of how money is created. The next criticism is fractional reserve banking contributes to excess debt and instability. This leads to bankruptcies and growing inequality. It strengthens the perceived need for perpetual and unsustainable economic growth.[100] While I can sympathize with this critique, it is more related to the level of the reserve requirement. The current level of about 10% is too low, thus contributing to instability. Finally, there is the Austrian Business Cycle Theory. It claims creating money with fractional reserve banking is more than destabilizing. It is a form of legalized financial fraud. Again, I can sympathize with them, but I do not advocate abandoning fractional reserve banking. None of these critiques offer a reasonable alternative.

Fractional reserve banking precedes the Fed. In the early 1860s, reserve requirements were as high as 25% for city banks and 15% for country banks.[101] Since its inception in 1913, the Federal Reserve Bank has had the authority to adjust the reserve requirement. It has done so from time to time. As recently as 1960, the reserve requirement for city banks was 18%.[102] For the next few decades, there was considerable experimentation. This was finally settled at 10% in 1992. The city bank and country bank designations were dropped in the late 1960s. Instead, the size of the bank became the basis of differentiation. Since then the Fed has adjusted the definitions of large and small banks as it saw fit.

The Fed also has the authority to create money and inject it into the economy (quantitative easing). It did this for the Great Recession of 2008. It is currently unwinding quantitative easing. It does that by taking back the money it lent to the government when the bonds mature. It could have elected to retire the government debt, basically giving the government money to pay for the maturing bonds and reducing the federal deficit. This may be inflationary if the economy is already strong, but if the economy is weak, it could provide the necessary stimulus. This would have created money indistinguishable from the money created by banks, but it is not based on debt. How should they use this authority?

I propose the Fed act to promote stability. They should increase the required reserve percentage over time. This, of course, would leave less money for banks to lend and would constrain the money supply. The Fed could then create money with quantitative easing. It could retire some government debt it owns if appropriate based on the state of the economy. This gives the Fed other tools to help safeguard the economy. Their preferred tool is to adjust interest rates. While the Fed's control over interest rates is indirect, it does control the Discount Rate and the Federal Funds Rate, which apply to transactions among banks. Banks respond to this by adjusting interest rates for deposits and loans. This makes banks slightly more attractive compared to government bonds. The government generally has to pay higher interest to sell its bonds.

When the Fed adjusts interest rates, it can have significant international adverse effects. For example, if the Fed raises interest rates, it generally strengthens the dollar. This means dollars become more expensive when purchased with foreign currency. With higher U.S. interest rates, foreign entities can get better returns in the U.S. This increases the demand for dollars and raises the cost of dollars in other currencies, thus strengthening the dollar. Many international loans use dollars. This includes ones to which the U.S. is not a party. So when the dollar strengthens, paying back those loans becomes more difficult. This increases the risk of default and tends to destabilize the global economy. The policy I propose would reduce both public and private debt and avoid potential debt bubbles.

This approach is not without potential problems. First, the banks will likely fight tooth and nail against such a policy. It will reduce their profitability. They will no longer have the gift of being almost the sole entity being able to create money. Creating money is the sovereign right of nations, not banks. The banks have ample resources to reinvent their business model based on new operating rules. The second risk is the Fed will create too much money, which could lead to runaway inflation. This could be the result of pressure from the government to keep the economy going. The federal government may pressure the Fed to help reduce the federal debt. The Fed was set up as an independent institution, and it has remained that way. The executive branch of government has recently challenged Fed independence. The Fed must stay strong and independent. On balance, the Fed acting more broadly to create a more stable system is necessary and beneficial.

CONCLUSION

These changes will not end instability. This instability is a fundamental part of our economic system. It may even be a fundamental part of our human nature. Still, these actions will make the system more stable. There is a bit of a trade-off between stability and growth. We are reaching the end of economic growth. This may be by reaching environmental limits or the limits of our economic system. Economic growth is no longer providing the progress we seek. We need to value stability and progress more than growth.

CHAPTER ELEVEN

SCALE

When I have talked about the size of the economy so far, I have used GDP as a proxy, but GDP is only a measure of the monetary value of the economy, a sum of all monetary transactions of final goods and services for a country. It covers a certain period of time, often a year. The scale is a measure of the physical size of the economic system. It is often measured as the throughput of the economy over a year. Throughput is the flow of raw materials from the environment, through the economy and back to the environment as waste.

As I have discussed, GDP is an imperfect measure of progress. It is also an imperfect measure of scale. GDP treats all monetary transactions of final goods the same. Filling your car's tank with gasoline and getting a haircut may have the same cost. They also may have the same effect on GDP, but their effects on scale and throughput are quite different. As far as living within the means of our environment is concerned, throughput is what matters.

The growth of the global economy has been slowing for decades. Throughput growth is slowing even faster. The energy intensity of the global GDP has been dropping at a rate of about 0.75% per year. Most of the energy we currently use comes from fossil fuels. These contribute to throughput. All that coal, oil, and natural gas comes from the environment to power the economy. The waste goes back into the environment. Most of the waste is carbon dioxide. There are also other products of combustion, so reducing energy intensity reduces throughput growth beyond the reduction in GDP growth.

Dealing with climate change will further reduce throughput, and to deal with climate change, we need to convert to renewable energy sources. Their production takes only minimal materials from the environment. Also, there are ongoing efforts to reduce the material content of GDP. The size of these efforts is difficult to even estimate, but they reduce the growth of throughput.

THRIVING WITH LESS THROUGHPUT

Reducing the growth of throughput is great news for the environment, but we will most likely have to actually stop and reverse the growth of throughput if we are to live within our environmental means. The scale of our global economy is already too large to sustain. Throughput will have to shrink to a sustainable size. There has been considerable effort made to understand what we need to thrive with reduced throughput. Tim Jackson provided a good summary in 2009 with the publication of *Prosperity without Growth? The transition to a sustainable economy.*[103] The Sustainable Development Commission funded this report, which proposes twelve areas of actions in three groups we need to prosper without growth. Here is a summary.

- Building a Sustainable Macro-Economy
  1. Developing macro-economic capability
  2. Investing in public assets and infrastructures
  3. Increasing financial and fiscal prudence
  4. Reforming macro-economic accounting
- Protecting Capabilities for Flourishing
  5. Sharing the available work and improving the work-life balance
  6. Tackling systemic inequality
  7. Measuring capabilities for flourishing
  8. Strengthening human and social capital
  9. Reversing the culture of consumerism
- Respecting Ecological Limits
  10. Imposing well-defined resource/emissions caps
  11. Implementing fiscal reform for sustainability
  12. Promoting technology transfer and international ecosystem protection.

The world was not ready to act on these in 2009. One of the sticking points was the report advocated imposing well-defined resource/emission caps (number ten above). This was seen as putting the brakes on economic growth. In 2009, the world was not ready for that. In fact, the world is still not ready for that, but one of the key points of this book is economic growth is slowing despite our most heroic actions to encourage it. Whether we like it or not, this is our future. The good news is there are ways to thrive with reduced throughput. Professor Jackson provided a view of how to do that. His recommended actions are consistent with many of those developed in this book. These will allow us to not only survive but build a world that better meets the needs of all of us.

MEASURING OUR WELL-BEING

As I have discussed, GDP is an imperfect economic measure. It does not distinguish between spending that improves our welfare and that which is harmful. There is no global consensus on a better measure, but there are many that have been proposed and used in various ways.[104] Why is how we measure important? There is an old saying attributed to business management consultant Peter Drucker, "If you can't measure it, you can't improve it." If we want to optimize our well-being and achieve a sustainable scale, we need a measuring tool that lets us know whether we are improving.

Before I look at alternatives, I will take a closer look at GDP's shortcomings. In 2011, Dēmos published a report called, *Beyond GDP, New Measures for a New Economy*. This looks at the shortcomings of GDP and outlines alternatives.[105] Dēmos is a "non-partisan public policy research and advocacy organization." It works toward four goals: a fair economy, a vibrant democracy, a public sector working toward the common good, and a responsible U.S. international engagement. These goals are much like those we are pursuing in this book. Here is a summary of the shortcomings they found.

1. GDP tells us nothing about how the benefits of economic growth are distributed among the population.
2. GDP does not distinguish between spending that is beneficial and that which is harmful.
3. GDP does not distinguish between spending that is beneficial and that which is defensive and protects against threats to our welfare, such as cleaning up pollution or military spending.

4. GDP tells us nothing about the sustainability of economic activity.
5. GDP is silent on the depletion of natural capital and ecosystem services.
6. GDP excludes non-market activities, such as household work and volunteering for charity organizations.
7. GDP does not account for social wellbeing, which includes poverty, life expectancy, and life satisfaction.

Or said another way, GDP ignores many of the bad effects of economic activity. It counts many of these as good things. It doesn't count many important good activities that are not transacted in markets. It ignores a fair distribution of wealth or income. We can address these shortcomings by fixing GDP or going beyond GDP with other measures, but it is not only a problem of fixing the methods. Rather, the deeper problem is the economic model lying behind GDP. Our over-reliance on GDP reinforces this problem. Our dependence on GDP requires an economic model devoted to growth at all costs. This should be a familiar theme by now. We need to change our economic measurement to provide better feedback and refocus public concern. This will bring new policy demands into the mainstream of debate. It will lead to better decision-making about the nation's future.

Of the many measures proposed, there are a few that seem to be gathering support. There is a list of alternate measures compiled in the Dēmos article referenced above. To me, the leading indicator at present is the GPI, the Genuine Progress Indicator. It uses a combination of twenty-six indicators in three areas: Economic, Environmental and Social. GPI has been calculated for seventeen countries and several U.S. states. It shows while GDP in the U.S. has increased 300% since 1970, GPI has been approximately flat. The Dēmos report has a great general discussion on measuring well-being. It also provides a good discussion of the GPI specifically. We need to start thinking more about GPI and less about GDP.

STABILIZING POPULATION

GDP growth is slowing despite all our efforts to encourage growth. Global population growth is also slowing. This population growth slowing is occurring most in developed countries and China. Many of these countries have birth rates below the replacement values. The developed countries made no real effort to reduce population growth. It happened spontaneously as effective birth control became available to most people in the 1960s. The education and empowerment of women reinforced this trend.

China, of course, implemented the one-child policy in 1979 as a means to limit population growth. This policy limited births to one per family. The exception was rural families could have a second child if the first one was a girl.[106] This policy was unnecessary. A reduction in the birth rate was already underway in China falling from about 5 births per woman in the early 1970s to 2.8 in 1979. The one-child policy reduced it to 1.5. The one-child policy accelerated a trend that was already underway. By limiting population growth and other policy changes, China was able to lift itself out of poverty. It became a large economic power though per capita income is still low.

But this one-child policy was coercive and had severe adverse consequences. The biggest was a reduction in the proportion of girls in the population. In China, male children are more desirable than female children. This preference is so strong that parents used sex-selective abortions to ensure a male child. If a female child was born, parents were so desperate for a boy that they resorted to female infanticide, abandonment, or neglect in order to have a second chance at having a boy baby.

Today there are more males in China than normal. There is now a generation of young men where many of them will be unable to find a wife. The one-child policy also had the effect of causing an unusually small generation. This accelerated the aging of the population. Now there are too few young people to support the elderly, and it will get worse. The one-child policy was repealed in 2015, and China has encouraged larger families, but Chinese families have been unresponsive. They have come to like small families. It is often difficult to put a genie back in the bottle.

Most of the developed world and China have birth rates near or below the replacement value, but there are a few large populations that don't. India with a population of 1.32 billion has a birth rate that has come down to 2.33 from almost 6 in 1970. The projected population for India is 1.7 billion by 2050.[107] That is an increase of almost 400 million people, more than the population of the United States. Pakistan with a population of 207 million has a birth rate of 3.6. Its projected population is 310 million by 2050, an increase of over 100 million people. The biggest projected increase in population is from Africa. It had 1.25 billion people in 2017.[108] Its projected population is 2.53 billion by 2050,[109] an increase of 1.3 billion people. The world population is 7.7 billion. The projected world population in 2050 is 9.8 billion, an increase of 2.1 billion people. Africa, India, and Pakistan with a combined population of 2.75 billion (36% of the total) will add 1.8 billion people by 2050 (85% of the total). The rest of the world will grow by "only" 0.3 billion people.

From all we know, feeding this many people in a sustainable manner will be very difficult if not impossible. Lifting them out of poverty will be even more difficult. Providing developed country lifestyles will be impossible because the resources of the planet will not allow it. In years with bad weather, we may see crop failures and famines. Unless we act with an aggressive plan and soon, climate change will increase the likelihood of years with bad weather. History shows us many isolated civilizations that exceeded the capacity of their environments did not end well. Some were able to recognize their limits and change their ways. Many did not and suffered a population collapse. If the whole world exceeds the world environment's capacity and suffers a collapse, it will be suffering on a scale we have never seen before.

These projections are not cast in stone. We can make choices to reduce population growth without being coercive. The easiest and most effective way to lower the birth rate is to make effective birth control available to anyone who wants it. This means providing it at a price they can afford, even free if necessary. All the available evidence indicates this is an effective and low-cost approach. By itself, it could be enough to bring the population to a sustainable scale. I cannot overstate the power and simplicity of this solution. So many of the solutions I propose are difficult, controversial, and limited in their scope or effectiveness. This one isn't any of those things, with the possible exception of being controversial.

There are those who oppose birth control on religious grounds. I respect their decision, and their right not to use contraceptives, but they don't have a right to impose their views on others. Other people oppose using taxpayer money to fund birth control on the grounds that the government has no right to tell us what to do in our own bedrooms, but making contraceptives available is completely different from forcing people to use them. Climate change and overpopulation are existential threats. What better purpose of a government than to protect its people from existential threats?

Another simple way to reduce the birth rate is to make business microloans to women in countries with high birth rates. This does many things. First, it makes women more equal partners in decisions about having children. In many of the countries with high birth rates, women have very little say in these matters. Also, business microloans provide more family income. This allows their children to be better nourished and better able to attend school. Girls who are better educated have more input into whether they have children as adults. Finally, by choosing businesses that provide beneficial products and services, the local community can also benefit from the loan.

The evidence of the effectiveness of these microloans is mixed. Some studies show a great success, but others don't. Providing money to a woman for a business doesn't make her a successful businessperson. It seems some people can be successful by getting a loan. For others, they need some guidance and support to be successful. The way these systems generally work is an organization crowdfunds individual loans.

One such organization is Kiva.[110] I will use them in this example. First, the applicant applies for the loan. Then the application goes through an underwriting and approval process. Once approved, the loan is posted on Kiva's website. Individuals then contribute to funding the loan in $25 increments. Once funded, the applicant receives the loan. Of course, there is interest charged on the loan. A local individual collects the repayment weekly. The loans are short term, generally a year or less.

The local representative is paid from the interest paid on the loan. The local representative is often more than a bill collector. They often provide some guidance and support. The quality of the local representative can make or break the success rate. As a loan is repaid, the money is credited to the lender's account. It can fund another loan or be returned to the lender. The default rate on Kiva loans is very low.

My wife and I have been making loans with Kiva for almost a decade. We have chosen to do something that works some of the time rather than doing nothing. We loan only to women selling beneficial products and services in countries with high birth rates. So far we have helped fund 173 loans. Kiva has lent over one billion dollars from 1.6 million lenders to 2.6 million borrowers.

THE FUTURE OF WORK

This section deals with how the slowing of population and economic growth affect how we work and how they affect economic inequality. Slowing population growth leads to aging populations, resulting in more old people and fewer young people. This makes governments and companies struggle to fund their commitments to pensioners.

Many companies reduced their pension liability by moving from defined benefit plans to defined contribution plans. In a defined benefit plan, companies promise to pay some amount for the rest of retirees' lives. In a defined contribution plan companies put a certain amount of money in a pot for employees. Employees may take it with them when they retire or leave the company.

Governments have been slow to address this issue. There are a limited number of options to resolve the problem. Governments can reduce benefits. They do this by increasing the retirement age or by reducing the amount they pay. Those who are receiving benefits or are soon to be receiving them fight both options. Organizations representing these people, including the AARP, lobby aggressively against these actions. The AARP is the American Association of Retired Persons. The other set of options is to increase the taxes on the young to pay the old. Two sets of people oppose this: young people who are struggling to get by and wealthy people who oppose all taxes. The latter of these two groups are well-funded to lobby against tax increases, so governments are in a box and debt continues to grow.

Because of the effect on the debt problem, this section could also have been in Chapter Ten, Financial Stability. Debt becomes excessive when the borrower can no longer service that debt. This leads to defaults. As government debt increases, the risk of default increases. Some small perturbation could make the government unable to service its debts.

Governments have a few options to deal with this eventuality. One is they could borrow more money as long as people are willing to lend it to them. It most likely will take higher interest rates on the loans to entice people to do that. This will only delay the problem and make it more difficult to solve the next time there is a perturbation. This action is only digging deeper the hole in which the government is. As the comedian and social commentator Will Rogers said, "When you find yourself in a hole, stop digging."

The size of the U.S. government debt makes default untenable because it can destabilize the world's financial system. It can then cause a severe recession or even depression. Another option national governments have is to print money. This is an option of last resort. If the amount of money printed is large enough, it will over time lead to inflation. Even if it is not large, the act of doing it will likely raise the public expectation of future inflation. The thinking is if the government does it once, it will do it again whenever it needs money.

Public inflation expectations are self-fulfilling. If people think inflation will get higher, it most likely will. When employees expect higher inflation, they more aggressively pursue raises. Companies seeing more pressure on wages start to raise their prices to maintain profits. Then you have higher inflation, fulfilling the prophecy. When inflation starts to rise, the central bank will increase interest rates to fight it. This makes it more difficult for the government to continue servicing its debt. Again, the government needs to stop digging.

Finally, this section could have fit in Chapter Nine, Fair Distribution. Economic growth continues to slow, and the population continues to increase. Also, the total factor productivity continues to increase. All these reduce the amount of labor required by each of us. The way things work now, this means unemployment will increase. This will cause economic inequality to get worse. The aging populations are causing the workforce to shrink. This helps, but governments will do as they almost must and increase the retirement age. That will increase the labor force and make the problem worse.

Finally, artificial intelligence threatens a large number of jobs, making un-employment worse. The problem is there is too much labor available for too little work, and the trend will get worse. This puts downward pressure on wages and increases economic inequality. So how do we get out of this mess?

Brian Czech is the founding president and executive director of CASSE (The Center for the Advancement of the Steady State Economy). In his book, *Supply Shock*,[111] he proposes modifying the Full Employment Act. The official name of this act is the Full Employment and Balanced Growth Act of 1978. Among its goals are "full employment and production, increased real income." "Balanced growth" is also among its goals. The government should cooperate with the private sector to achieve this. It also "mandates the Board of Governors of the Federal Reserve to establish a monetary policy that maintains long-run growth, minimizes inflation, and promotes price stability."[112] This formalizes the federal government's goal of promoting long term growth.

But with our future being low growth or a steady state, this is no longer appropriate. Brian proposes changing the name to the Full and Sustainable Employment Act. It might become known as the Full Seas Act, a jab at the rising tide analogy. The goal of "increased real income" would become "sta-bilized real income." The goal of "balanced growth" would become "efficient allocation of land, labor, and capital." I would add, freeing the Fed from the mandate to maintain long-term growth. While I support Brian's proposal, I advocate a more comprehensive solution as the following discussion shows.

The retirement age at which benefits are available is increasing slowly. In the United States, the retirement age at which a reduced Social Security retirement benefit is available is age sixty-two. Full benefits are available when retirement occurs at age sixty-six years and two months for those born in 1955. It is increasing toward sixty-seven years for those born in 1960 and retiring in 2027. Early retirement will still be at age sixty-two but with a greater reduction. We must speed up and extend this to manage the debt problem.

Of course, encouraging people to retire later makes the problem of too much available labor worse. There are a couple of approaches to address this. One would be to reduce the standard workweek from forty hours. This is not a radical idea. Here are some thoughts from an article from *The Economist* on the subject.[113] In the 1870s the average workweek was between sixty and seventy hours. Since then it has been gradually reduced, but this reduction has not been consistent over time nor has it been consistent among countries.

In 1970, the annual time worked per worker in the U.S. was about 1,900 hours. This was less than Germany or France, which were at about 2,000 hours. It was more than Britain, which was about 1,800 hours. By 2016 the annual time worked in the U.S. was 1,800 hours, Germany was 1,400 hours, France was 1,500 hours, and Britain was 1,600. So the U.S. went from second lowest to highest hours worked among this group. Also, note the inequality ranking matches the hours worked ranking. Higher hours worked correlates to higher inequality. Of course, this doesn't prove causality. It just says the U.S. has higher inequality and more work hours than the other countries in the above group.

There would have to be a method developed to manage how far and how fast to change the standard work week. It should also be done in a way that does not reduce employee earnings. One goal would be to reduce the debt associated with retirement benefits to a manageable level. It would also have a goal to ensure wages increase toward a level that provides the desired level of economic inequality. As I discussed in Chapter Three, "Inequality," a Gini Coefficient for wealth of 0.55 may be a reasonable target. This would encourage companies to hire more people rather than pay overtime.

Another way to reduce the available labor would be to encourage companies to allow reduced hours for any employee. These could be used as a transition by those employees approaching retirement. It could also be used by those who have health problems, those who need more time to care for loved ones, or those who just want more time to do what is important to them. While this would reduce the available labor, it is not without its challenges. It is more difficult for companies to manage workloads when a job is divided among multiple people. There needs to be some limits on the size of the reduction allowed. I suspect a reduction of 50% is about the maximum that can be managed. Another question is how much of a reduction in pay would be required. Is it just a reduction in pay proportional to the hours worked, or is there also some reduction in benefits? In the end, I suspect this approach is too disruptive and difficult to manage to be widely applied.

So our tools to manage debt related to retirement benefits and the oversupply of labor are to increase the retirement age and reduce the standard work week.

ANOTHER FED ROLE

As I have discussed, the Federal Reserve System has a big and difficult job. It has recently seen its main job as balancing between inflation and unemployment. The Fed seems to be trying to make unemployment as low as possible without igniting inflation. In Chapter Ten, I made the case the Fed should also be doing its part to make our financial system more stable. This includes changing the rules and managing debt. This is a role the Fed does reluctantly when the financial system appears to be in dire straits. For example, it did so when the financial system was crumbling in 2008.

Now, I want to suggest one more goal for the Fed. That is to have a target for economic growth other than as high as possible. Global growth has been slowing for decades. The data show and it is my expectation economic growth will approach zero by the end of the 21st century. I have also shown collapse is possible. If this happens, economic growth could be negative for an extended period of time. The more we push for economic growth at all costs, the more likely is a collapse. The best way to minimize that chance is to start actively slowing economic growth. Of all the policy options I have discussed, this one most likely has the least support. This is because most people cannot envision a world where there is no economic growth. If they have given it any thought at all, they think it would be a dismal place. I have a different vision of a world without economic growth. The policies in this book are a start toward a world that is more economically fair and stable, and people have more time to do what is important to them. These policies will also lead to a healthy and stable environment. Personal fulfillment and happiness will define prosperity and growth.

One way the Fed could set an economic growth limit would be to use the expected growth based on long-term trends as a maximum. This long-term growth is thought to be close to the maximum the economy can sustain without increasing inflation. This is close to what the Fed does now, but it would slow down the economy when it first gets above the growth maximum rather than waiting for inflation to exceed its target. Besides slightly putting the brakes on economic growth, it would limit the boom and bust cycles. It would also make asset and debt bubbles less likely. This would be a beneficial extension of Fed goals.

PART III: TRANSITION

Part III will provide some guidelines that could help us get the policies outlined in Part II implemented. This will not be easy. It is hard to imagine the partisan fighting in Washington will stop long enough for our government to function as we would like. Still, change sometimes happens with lightning rapidity when the conditions are right.

CHAPTER TWELVE

IMPLEMENTING POLICIES

The best policies in the world do no good unless they are put in place. Policy wonks can celebrate their work, social media can light up with excitement, and cable news from both the left and right can cheer, but if it is not implemented, it is all for naught. As I write this, the United States government is partially shut down. It is the longest shutdown we have endured. A fight over President Trump's southern border wall caused this one. The President wants it, but Congress does not, even some of his own party. Given the dysfunction of our government, it is hard to imagine the kind of deliberation, debate, and compromise needed to enact the kind of policies advocated in this book. Still, there are reasons to be hopeful.

VOTING

A June 2018 poll conducted by Pew Research Center found 77% of Americans say, "There should be limits on the amount of money individuals and groups can spend on campaigns." The same poll also found that 65% of Americans agree, "New laws could be written that would be effective in reducing the role of money in politics."[114] A December 2018 poll conducted by Politico found 58% of Americans (including 34% of Republicans) accept "that human activity is the main cause of climate change."[115] A survey conducted by Ipsos in August 2018 found 64% of Americans "believe the U.S. economy is rigged to the advantage of the rich and powerful"[116] A June 2016 poll conducted by the Pew

Research Center found the economy was the top issue in affecting voting decisions; "84% of registered voters say that the issue of the economy will be very important to them in making their decision about who to vote for in the 2016 presidential election."[117] The same poll, which considered fourteen issues, did not even include climate change, so while most Americans accept human activity is the main cause of climate change, addressing it wasn't even a real option in the 2016 presidential election.

The economy, however, was the top issue. Seeing this, one would think that should have been an overwhelming mandate to unrig the economy. If the 2016 election taught us anything, it is polling is tricky business. The exact wording of the poll can make a huge difference, and interpreting the results is more art than science. The fact that eighty-four percent of Americans said the issue of the economy was very important doesn't mean there is a consensus or even a majority agreement on what should be done. Fifty-eight percent of Americans accept human-caused climate change, but this doesn't mean they support doing something about it.

What we need to do is take the energy around the economy and focus it on effective policies that unrig it. We need to provide effective policies to combat climate change to the 58% of Americans who accept it is human-caused. These groups need to accept each other to be successful. There is an array of issues affecting how we vote on which members of these groups will disagree, sometimes even passionately.

Let's explore some of these issues. Like it or not, racial issues still evoke passionate emotions. America may be a great melting pot, but it is an incomplete one. Even though we may be making progress, it is a slow and uneven process with advances and setbacks. Healthcare reform is badly needed in our country. We spend more on healthcare than any other country but have less than average developed country outcomes. Any form of gun control enrages many Americans. The National Rifle Association has a hair trigger to anything that sounds like gun control, yet we must live with more gun violence and mass shootings than most developed countries. Immigration is another emotional issue as the current government shutdown confirms. To this list, we could also add abortion, LGBTQ rights, and other issues.

We need to set these issues aside. If we think of people with whom we disagree as morally inferior, bad people with whom we can't work, we all lose. We need to work together on the issues where most of us agree: unrigging the economy and combating climate change.

The members of the public who support unrigging the economy and combating climate change need to work together, but our elected representatives need to do the same. They need to feel public support for addressing these issues. This can help them set aside their differences on other issues. The fossil fuel industry and wealthy elites will resist this with the full force of their resources. To limit their effectiveness, it may be necessary to enact meaningful campaign finance reform. At least, it would be better to enact meaningful campaign finance reform first.

Polls suggest addressing economic fairness and the climate crisis are important to the American people. We need to support our elected representatives who give these issues a high priority. We need to be crystal clear our support is contingent on that. We should also support elected representatives who support campaign finance reform. A unified public acting in this way is the greatest fear of the fossil fuel industry and wealthy elites. They would prefer to see us fighting among ourselves rather than acting as a unified force on the issues important to most of us. If we can do this, we can address economic fairness and the climate crisis.

When politicians treat rivals as enemies to vanquish, our democracy starts to die. Instead, they should treat them as rivals on this particular issue. They may be their allies tomorrow on a different issue. Treating rivals as enemies leads to dysfunction. This puts democracy on a path that leads to its own destruction. It opens the door for autocrats to rise to power. It weakens the rule of law. The case for this thinking is best presented by Steven Levitsky and Daniel Ziblatt in their book, *How Democracies Die*.[118] They are two Harvard professors of government. They say our democracy has not survived for almost 250 years because of our constitution or laws, even though they admit both are important, but rather because of norms of behavior that developed over time.

These unwritten norms require rival representatives treat each other with respect. They should use the full strengths of their positions only as a last resort. These norms encourage the kind of deliberation, debate, and compromise that allow democracies to thrive. Unfortunately, these norms have been eroded over the last few decades. This erosion has accelerated in the last few years.

Hopefully, I have been successful in convincing you of the policies I have advocated in this book. When voting I ask you give significant weight to candidates who support these policies. Candidates who earn our votes should support campaign finance reform. They should support unrigging the economy.

This means they should support many of the policies discussed in Chapters Nine and Ten. They should also support effective solutions to the climate crisis discussed in Chapter Eight. Finally, they should be willing to deliberate, debate, and compromise to strengthen our democracy. I know this is a big ask. I can only do my best to convince you these policies will result in a better America and a better world and ask you to vote your conscience.

WRITING TO ELECTED OFFICIALS

Writing to our elected officials is a time-honored way to get help on a particular issue. A good, short, physical letter to an official who represents you followed up with a phone call is most effective. Don't write to anybody who does not represent you. Emails usually get a canned response, if that. Canned letters from online organizations are the least effective. Yet they do serve a useful purpose. When combined with letters from many others, they give elected officials an idea of how many people are concerned about your issue. They also increase the influence of the organization that puts the letter online. If you support what the organization is doing, this helps your cause in a roundabout way. This is covered more in the next section on Non-Governmental Organizations. *ThoughtCo* has some good tips on how best to write a letter.[119]

Unfortunately, each representative represents about 700,000 people and most senators represent millions. Getting your issues heard is not easy. Getting the desired action is even harder. If you want to influence your representative, you need a plan to enlist the support of many other people. One way to start is to build relationships with local representatives who share your concern. They are likely to be easier to access and may know the elected official you are trying to influence. They will add credibility to your request. They can also provide direction on the best way to proceed. A petition with one hundred signatures might be more effective. A *Quora* article gives some insight into how an elected official's office works and how they may be influenced.[120]

Alas, this is more effort than most people can handle. They have a day job and a family and friends. There is only so much time and energy they can allocate to political activism. I get that. I spent thirty-nine years in demanding engineering jobs and raised two kids with my wife.

Besides voting, there are other things we can do to support these policies. One of them is to support Non-Governmental Organizations that advocate for these policies. There are many NGOs for all kinds of issues. To simplify this a bit, I will discuss a few. For climate change, I support The Climate Change Reality Project.[121] Their mission is, "...to catalyze a global solution to the climate crisis by making urgent action a necessity across every level of society." That's a big mission, but they are a big and growing organization. They seem well-organized and well-run.

If population growth issues speak to you, I support Kiva for microloans. I focus on women with beneficial products and services in countries with high fertility rates.[122]

If you're concerned about a sustainable scale, I recommend CASSE, the Center for the Advancement of the Steady State Economy.[123] Here is their mission statement: "The mission of CASSE is to advance the steady state economy, with stabilized population and consumption, as a policy goal with widespread public support. We pursue this mission by educating citizens, organizations, and policymakers on the conflict between economic growth and (1) environmental protection, (2) ecological and economic sustainability, and (3) national security and international stability; promoting the steady state economy as a desirable alternative to economic growth; studying the means to establish a steady state economy." In the interest of transparency, I am the volunteer Chairman of the CASSE Upstate South Carolina Chapter.

Another organization in this vein is the Post Growth Institute; its mission is, "to inspire, mobilize, and support individuals, businesses, and communities in transitioning to a thriving, sustainable society based on the continuous circulation of resources within ecological limits." I have written a couple of guest blog articles for them on energy, climate change and the economy, and inequality.[124, 125]

Finally, there does not seem to be one NGO that focuses on unrigging the United States economy. There are many that focus on individual issues, many of which I have discussed. There are also some that are broader in one of two ways. Either they are global in nature or cover a wide range of social justice issues. I can offer a couple that may be a place to start. The first one is The Fight Inequality Alliance. It is a global organization with partners in many countries.[126] One of their partners in the United States is the Center for Economic and Social Rights.[127] The other is Inequality.org.[128] This is another international organization with information and policies to fight inequality.

I encourage you to investigate these organizations and support any that speak to you. You can support them by signing letters they compose to representatives, and you can support them financially. To the extent that they align with your interests, you can use them to keep up to date on issues important to you.

Chapter Thirteen

Conclusions

We have covered a lot of ground in this book at a pretty rapid pace. There have been many conclusions drawn. It may be helpful to summarize the discussions before reaching any overarching conclusions. In Part I, I explored several related issues we need to address. The discussion on climate change focused on why it is so hard to accept the reality of human-caused climate change and why it is even more difficult to act to mitigate it. Part of the problem is there is uncertainty. The fossil fuel industry uses this uncertainty to cast doubt on our understanding.

Beyond the uncertainty, climate change challenges our whole prevailing worldview. That worldview says economic growth equals prosperity, and more is better. Resolving climate change requires rebuilding our entire energy delivery system. The rebuilt system will have to reduce carbon dioxide emissions enough to avoid the worst consequences of climate change. It also requires we change our prevailing worldview. The new worldview says once we have enough, more doesn't increase prosperity much. It may actually be counterproductive.

Next, I showed global energy use and GDP are highly correlated. As GDP goes up, energy use also goes up. The correlation is not one-to-one. Energy efficiency improvements have reduced the energy intensity (energy/GDP) of the economy, but so far these improvements have been much less than the growth in GDP. I also found the stunning result that global growth in GDP has been slowing from 5.4% in the 1960s to an expected 2.2% in the 2010s. It is expected to approach zero over the next century or so. Slowing of economic growth is not something that might happen in the future. It has been happening for the last fifty years and is expected to continue. This realization represents a frontal attack on our prevailing worldview that more is better.

I explored economic inequality. I found economic inequality in the United States is one of the highest among the developed countries. I also showed higher economic inequality correlates with a long list of social maladies. Polls show Americans prefer a much lower economic inequality, lower than any country has achieved, yet making economic inequality more like other developed countries can reduce social maladies. There are two ways to achieve lower economic inequality. One is to tax the rich and transfer money to the poor. The other is to level the playing field by creating equality of opportunity. Equality of opportunity is a core American value, but in practice, the playing field is anything but level. Economic mobility is low. Those born into rich or poor families are likely to stay that way as adults.

I analyzed trends in population. I saw the global population is already above the sustainable carrying capacity of the planet. There is considerable uncertainty in population projections. This leads to a wide range of possibilities. The latest United Nations projection has 95% confidence limits for the population in the year 2100 of between 9.6 and 13.2 billion people. Even this doesn't capture the extent of the uncertainty. It assumes current trends continue. There is also the possibility of population collapse. This may be due to overexploitation of natural resources. This type of collapse is common in the animal world. There have been several examples of isolated human civilizations that have collapsed. Our global civilization is isolated to this planet and is susceptible to collapse.

There is some good news. I showed global population growth is slowing. Fertility rates have dropped or are dropping rapidly everywhere but in Africa. Many countries have fertility rates below the replacement value. To the extent that we can stop global population growth, we can reduce the chances of collapse. One other characteristic of a population is the age distribution. As the fertility rate drops the population ages. This results in more elderly people and fewer working age people. It challenges our ability to care for the elderly.

Part I ended with a discussion of a few other constraints. I looked at how the world is awash in debt partly due to pensions for the elderly. This debt can become excessive and cause severe recessions and depressions. This led to a discussion of financial stability. Our economic and financial system cycles between expansions and recessions. In our effort to maintain economic growth, we have created a system that is more unstable than is healthy or necessary. In the United States, this is partly due to the influence of money in our political system. I discussed how our campaign finance laws allow undue influence by large corporations and wealthy individuals. Finally, I reviewed how GDP is measured. I looked at some of its shortcomings and some alternatives that are better measures of well-being.

The discussions in Part I can leave one overwhelmed, especially if one has had limited previous exposure to some of these topics. It can leave one with a dismal view of where we are and where we are going. There are many policies that have been developed that can improve our lot. I explored those in Part II.

Part II began with a discussion of what we want. I discussed Maslow's hierarchy of needs. These include Physiological needs (food, water, shelter, sex, rest, etc.), Security and Safety, Belonging (intimate relationships, friends, and family), Esteem (accomplishment, recognition, prestige, etc.), and Fulfillment (purpose, achieving full potential, happiness, etc.). These seem to make sense to most people. I added a few needs to those including a need for a sense of fairness.

We know the world is not always fair, but to the extent possible, we want to feel it is not rigged against us. As part of our security, we need a stable economy. Finally, to achieve these needs we must have a stable and healthy environment. These things can be achievable for most of us if we as a society make the right choices.

One of the first choices we as Americans need to make is to reduce the influence of money in our politics. First I discussed the challenges of campaign finance reform. A big challenge is to avoid infringing on First Amendment rights. There are some innovative options that are thought not to infringe on these rights. I advocated for voting with dollars, where each citizen gets a monetary voucher. It can be used only to support political candidates of their choice. There are some fine points that are constructed to ensure constitutionality, but we will never know for sure until it survives a Supreme Court challenge.

Next, I discussed eliminating gerrymandering, the defining of districts for political gain. So far efforts to limit gerrymandering have been ineffective. The biggest problem seems to be the difficulty in determining if a plan is fair or gerrymandered. Recently, mathematicians have developed a method to assess the fairness of a plan. It involves checking a representative sample of all possible plans. The lower courts have already looked favorably on this approach.

Finally, I discussed eliminating the revolving door. This is where people move from industry to government and back. Unfortunately, this is often where the expertise lies, but it influences government decisions to be more favorable to business. The solution is to fund congress and the executive branch so they may develop their own independent in-house expertise. This will limit the revolving door.

Most economists agree the most efficient way to address climate change is to put a price on carbon dioxide emissions. This lets the market find the most efficient way to reduce emissions. This can be either a tax or a cap and trade system. Either system can work if done well, but a tax is easier to get right. It can be revenue neutral by, for example, providing an equal refund to all citizens. Such a tax to limit the global temperature increase to 2° C from preindustrial times could start in 2020 at about $0.04 per gallon of gasoline. This tax would then increase linearly to about $2.59 (in 2015 dollars) per gallon of gasoline by 2045 and then would be reduced over time. It appears to be already too late to limit the global temperature increase to 1.5° C without drastic measures. Another thing we must do is to end subsidies to the fossil fuel industry. Globally, they are in the range of $775 billion to $1 trillion per year. These subsidies are sending the exact opposite message to the market. In other words, they encourage increasing carbon dioxide emissions. They must be eliminated.

In Chapter Nine, "Fair Distribution," I discussed a long list of policies to reduce inequality. These include inheritance taxes, progressive income tax, which can help fund other reforms. The other reforms are a universal basic income, minimum wage, addressing excessive chief executive officer pay, eliminating subsidies, reforming patent laws, strengthening antitrust laws, and improving trade agreements. This long list is necessary to help create a level playing field. It took us decades to get to the tilted playing field we now have, and it will likely take us decades to fix it. This list is a good starting point. The items on the list have been discussed to some degree. Some of them need to revert to earlier laws while other laws need to be strengthened. A few are completely new.

The wealthy elites will fight these changes with all their considerable resources. The countervailing force will have to come back strong to achieve these changes. There are reasons to think it will be successful. These policy changes are in the interest of the majority of the American people. There is a new generation of politicians that senses addressing these issues can help them get elected. They are intelligent, articulate, and passionate about these issues. It is likely some of them will excite the electorate and rise to power. If enough of them do, there is a real chance for change.

I discussed the financial stability of our economic system. Cycles of recession and expansion are inherent in our economic system. Our efforts to achieve economic growth at any cost have made the system more unstable. Slower economic growth has made it more difficult to avoid recessions. For all these reasons, we need to make our economic system more stable and robust. Some of our financial institutions are too big to fail, so from time to time, we bail them out. This creates a moral hazard that increases risk-taking. It increases the chances they will need to be bailed out again. To break this loop, we need to break up these too-big-to-fail institutions and companies. Any bailout package must include breaking them up into pieces that can be allowed to fail. Too big to fail is too big to exist.

Instability in our stock markets can sometimes cause instability in the economic system. This instability is often caused by frequent stock trading, some of which is automated. To combat this, we need to encourage longer-term investment rather than shorter-term speculation. One way to do this is with a transaction tax. A small percentage transaction tax can encourage a longer-term perspective and a more stable stock market. Finally, the Fed should increase the reserve requirements of banks over time. This takes back some of the government's sovereign right to create money. These actions will not end the business cycle but can temper it and make it less destructive.

I finished Part II with a discussion of scale. Transitioning to a sustainable scale will be the most challenging change. Today there is little support for this transition. If climate change is an indirect threat to the worldview of more is better, transitioning to a sustainable scale is a direct frontal attack. Like climate change, the excessive scale is an existential threat. Converting from fossil fuels to renewable energy sources can address the climate crisis, but there are many other constraints. These include available fresh water, arable land, and certain minerals. These are only addressed by reducing the throughput of the economy to a sustainable scale. Transitioning to a sustainable scale requires developing a compelling new worldview. This worldview says we can all live better, more fulfilling lives while keeping the scale of our economic system within natural limits. In this book, I have taken the first few tentative steps toward that vision.

In Part III I touched on how to put in place these policies. I showed how polls say Americans are concerned about the economy and climate change. I also showed how many of us think the economy is rigged to the advantage of the wealthy elite. The policies discussed in this book address those issues. I discussed when we vote, we need to focus our decisions on these important issues. We need to avoid hot-button issues. Our representatives must deliberate, debate and compromise. They need to treat each other with respect. These are the characteristics that strengthen our democracy.

I discussed how writing to representatives has little effect unless we can enlist many people to join us. Calling their offices or enlisting local politicians who support your view can help. Few of us can afford the time or energy for this level of activism. Another way to get many people to influence representatives is by supporting Non-Governmental Organizations that support your view. I reviewed some options.

After exploring all these issues, what conclusions can we draw? In discussing the wide scope of these issues, I came to many conclusions. To help get your minds around them, I have tried to consolidate and clarify them. The list below is my attempt to help see, understand, and remember the main points of the discussion.

1. It is important for us to understand, for many issues, our choices can influence outcomes. Our economic, political, and legal systems are a result of choices made over centuries. These systems can be changed by the choices we make. While our choices can affect the outcomes of natural systems, we cannot change the laws of nature.

2. The size of the economy drives our energy use. Burning fossil fuels for that energy causes climate change. The growth of our global economy has been slowing for decades. I expect global economic growth to be about zero by the end of this century. With lower economic growth, economic inequality and stability become worse. We must solve these issues together.

3. Our view of the world affects the choices we make. Many of us believe in some version of the more is better worldview. This is so even

though we know in our hearts more stuff is not what is important. We need to embrace a worldview that says once we have enough, more is not better.

4. Human-caused climate change is already changing our world and not for the better. We are starting to get a glimpse of the crazy climate we are creating. It includes more droughts and wildfires, more severe hurricanes and heat waves, and glaciers melting causing sea level to rise. It even includes the occasional polar vortex that wanders south from the Arctic. The jet stream is no longer strong enough to keep it there. The best way to address climate change is to enact a revenue-neutral tax on carbon emissions. That tax can start small and increase with time to about 2050. Then it can be relaxed over time. The market can work out the most efficient way to meet our energy needs without carbon emissions.

5. Most Americans believe the wealthy elite have rigged our economic system to their advantage. This results in severe economic inequality. This inequality is associated with a long list of social maladies. These include worse health, life expectancy, drug problems, violence, mental illness, and obesity. It also includes higher rates of imprisonment and teenage birth rates. Finally, it includes lower social and economic mobility.

While our challenges are many and complex and the opponents powerful, we have the knowledge and countervailing force to make better choices. This allows us to construct a fairer economic system and mitigate the climate crisis, creating better lives for all. In the end, I can only provide a dim glimpse of a better future that we can choose to create.

Appendix

In this appendix, I develop a model to project GDP based on projecting the individual factors in the Solow equation. This will provide more support to the idea of using the logistic function discussed in Chapter Two.

Rather than try to fit GDP data, it is better to project each of the factors that go into determining the GDP then use those to estimate future GDP. Beyond that, a couple of improvements to the Solow model are desirable. I used the number of employed individuals instead of the total population. I also used education level to augment employed individuals as described in Acemoglu 2009.[13] Economists use education level with capital and labor to calculate the economic output.

The Mankiw–Romer-Weil version of the Solow model can be used to include the education level of the workforce. This breaks the Solow model into three parts: 1) capital stock, 2) human capital, and 3) the product of total factor productivity and labor. Daron Acemoglu[13] (an authority on economic growth) advocates this as an improved approach, and this is what I used. Let's see how this would work.

The equation for the Mankiw–Romer-Weil version of the Solow equation is shown below in Equation A.1.

$$Y = K^{\alpha} \; H^{\beta} \; (L_e \, A)^{(1-\alpha-\beta)} \tag{A.1}$$

Where,

Y = the economic output or GDP per year,

K = the capital stock,

α = the output elasticity of the capital stock

H = the global index of human capital per person,

β = the output elasticity of the human capital stock,

L_e = the global number of persons employed.

A = the total factor productivity,

Here α is 0.36, and β is 0.26 based on work by Mankiw, Romer, and Weil and summarized in Acemoglu.[13] When I calculate the total factor productivity for the available data based on equation A.1, one thing is immediately obvious. The value is much lower than it was using the simple Solow equation. We cannot compare the total factor productivities calculated by different methods. With capital and labor (including human capital) the total factor productivity contributes to economic output. Part of the total factor productivity represents the effectiveness of the workforce. This is usually expressed as years of education and/or relevant experience.

There doesn't seem to be any way to measure the total factor productivity itself. Rather, it is calculated once labor, capital, and economic output are known, so we need to compare the projected GDPs. To use this approach to project the GDP, I needed to project the individual factors of the Mankiw–Romer-Weil version of the Solow equation.

First, I needed a projection of the global index of human capital per person. The Penn World Table has this information for each country. To get the world index of human capital I use a weighted average. First, I sum the number of persons employed for all the countries to get world data. Then I multiply the human capital per person by the number of persons employed for each country. This product is then summed for all the countries. Finally, I divide this sum by the total global number of persons employed to get a weighted average. This is the global index of human capital per person.

When evaluating the global index of human capital per person from 1960 to 2014, I found the data is linear. Using the linear projection, the global index of human capital per person would exceed the U.S. level by 2100. This doesn't make sense. The U.S. and other developed countries are reaching a maximum. This information can help with the global logistic curve fit, yet mature economies seem to be approaching a limit. Germany has been about constant for ten years to 2014. The U.S. is the country with the highest 2014 index of human capital per person. Modeling the U.S. index of human capital data with a logistic curve fit is more appropriate. With that fit, the midpoint is the year 1935. The maximum index of the U.S. human capital per person is about 14% higher than it is today. It may be possible to achieve higher levels of education, but for whatever reason, the education level in developed countries is slowing.

I assume the limit for developed countries applies to the world. The logistic curve for the global index of human capital per person then results in a better fit. The midpoint is 1984 and the maximum achieved in about the year 2300 is about 71% higher than where it is today. It also projects it will take until about the year 2300 for the rest of the world to reach the maximum the U.S. is approaching. In fact, the world is not expected to reach today's U.S. level until the year 2150. Slowing human capital growth appears to be another factor that may be contributing to the slowing of GDP growth. Graph A.1 may help understand this.

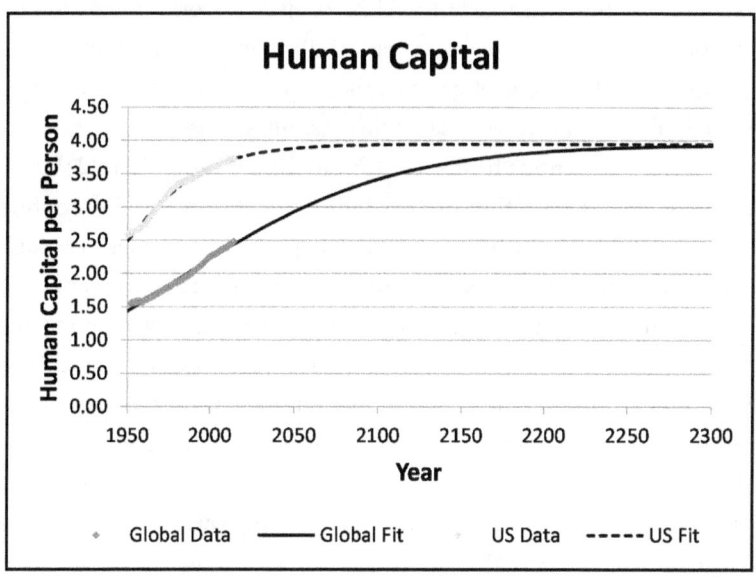

Graph A.1. The US and Global Human Capital Data and Projections

Next, I needed a projection of the global number of employed persons. First, I had to determine the global logistic curve for the percent of people employed. Then I multiplied that by the population to get the number of employed persons. The U.N. projects the long term trend in the global percentage of people ages 15 through 64 to approach 52% by the year 2300 (U.N. 2004[14]).

From the Penn World Table data, one can calculate the percentage of the global population employed. In 1960 this was 37.1% and has been increasing to 45.0% in 2011. When I apply a logistic curve fit to this data, I set the maximum to 52% of the global population employed, which matches the 52% of people who are in the 15 through 64 age group projected by the U.N. These are consistent since not all people in the 15 through 64 age group will work, and some people outside of ages 15 through 64 will work. With this information, I chose a logistic curve to project the percentage of the global population employed. The midpoint of this curve is the year 1919, and the maximum in the year 2300 is about 17% higher than where it is today.

To get the number of people employed, a population model is needed. There has been a lot of work done to develop historic population data for about the last 2,000 years. There has been a similar amount of work to project the data into the future. In 2004 the U.N. projected world population to the year 2300. The medium projection was 9 billion in the year 2300, but there was a huge variability. To capture that, they gave a range of projections from 2.3 to 36.4 billion. This is so variable that it is almost useless.

The latest projections from the U.N. in 2019[129] go only to 2100. They project an average population of 10.9 billion in 2100 with 95% confidence limits of 9.4 to 12.6 billion. The population logistic curve model uses the 2019 average projection. The results of the logistic curve fit are a midpoint of 2004, and the maximum is about 13.0 billion. This is 75% higher than where it is today. It projects 11.4 billion for the year 2100, which is within the U.N. confidence limits. To get the projected global number of people employed, the global projected percentage of people employed is multiplied by the global projected population.

Since the growth of the percent of people employed and the number of people are both leveling off, this contributes to the slowing of economic growth. One of the causes of the leveling of the percent of people employed is the percent of women in the workforce. In 1960 about 40% of U.S. women were in the workforce. That increased to a maximum of 60% in 1999. Since then it has come down a bit to 57% in 2016. Other developed countries seem to be following a similar trend but range from about 40% in Italy to 70% in Sweden.[10] So since 1960, a large number of women have entered the workforce, which increased the economic growth until about 1999, but that trend is slowing. Since 1999, the percent of women employed is not growing as fast. This slowing may partly explain the reduced growth shown above, but as I will show, there are some other factors as well.

The next piece of the puzzle is to estimate the capital stock. In economics, capital stock consists of the physical assets that help us supply products and services. This includes things like machinery and buildings, but it also includes infrastructure: such things as the transportation system, the electric grid, and the water supply. The Penn World Table provides this data from 1960 to 2014. I modeled the global capital stock data with a logistic curve. The best fit midpoint is the year 2036, and the maximum global capital stock is about 2.2 times higher than it is today.

The exponential curve is indistinguishable from the logistic curve over the time frame of the data, but the exponential curve has the unfortunate property of increasing at an increasing rate forever. David Attenborough said, "Anyone who thinks that you can have infinite growth on a planet with finite resources is either a madman or an economist." The capital stock is often measured in dollars, but they are physical assets that need resources to produce and maintain.

The total factor productivity can be reanalyzed with the growth model shown in Equation A.1. First, the total factor productivity is calculated over the range of 1960 to 2017. I now had data for all the factors. I needed the GDP. Good GDP data is available over that range from the World Bank.[15] The other factors have good data from only 1960 to 2014, but it is safe to project them for three years.

The resulting total factor productivity data is quite variable. There is rapid growth from 1960 to about 1973 then stagnation to about 1990. Finally, there was growth again to 2017. There is a surprisingly small slump during the recession years 2008 and 2009. Now, curves can be fit through this data. There is little difference among linear, second order (parabolic), exponential and logistic fits. The parabolic and logistic curves fit a little better than the exponential. They show a slight downward curve to the trend matching the data. The linear fit by definition shows no curve. The exponential fit curves in the opposite direction from the data. The parabolic fit and the logistic fit match are similar until the year 2200. At that point, the parabolic curve reaches a maximum and starts going back down. This makes no sense. The logistic curve smoothly approaches its maximum, so this is the curve I chose to use. The midpoint of the total factor productivity logistic curve is the year 1977, and the maximum is about 22% higher than today.

Now I can project all the factors. I can project GDP by calculating it using Equation A.1 and all the projected factors. It might be helpful to summarize the various curve fits used. These are shown below in Table A.1. The equations chosen are identified. If you are uncomfortable with the equations, you may skip it.

Variable	Fit Type	Equation	R²	Comment
Capital Stock	Logistic	$Y=1414/(1+e^{-0.0474*(x-2037)})$	99.8%	Chosen to avoid unlimited growth
Human Capital	Logistic	$Y=3.946/(1+e^{-0.0162*(x-1984)})$	97.4%	Chosen to match US projected maximum
Employed % of Population	Logistic	$Y=0.520/(1+e^{-0.0194*(x-1920)})$	96.4%	Chosen to match working age % max
Population	Logistic	$Y=13.0/(1+e^{-0.0204*(x-2005)})$	98.6%	"S" shaped population data
Total Factor Productivity	Logistic	$Y=62.7/(1+e^{(-0.0371*(x-1978)})$	86.4%	Chosen since quadratic falls off after 2200

Table A.1. Summary of curve fits needed to project GDP.

Remember, R^2 is the coefficient of determination and is a measure of variability. In this case, it explains how well the chosen equation explains the variability in the data. It varies from 0% to 100%, where 0% means it doesn't explain the variability at all. One hundred percent means it explains the data completely. While the chosen equations are not always the best fit, they are about as good as the best alternative. The chosen forms all have some desirable features that make them better choices. The R^2 values are important because they show these equations form a good fit to the data and a reasonable long term projection of global GDP. One that needs a little more discussion is the total factor productivity, which has a significantly lower R^2 than the rest. This is caused by short term variability in GDP that this economic model doesn't capture well. Since we are focused on long term projections, this does not concern us.

In Chapter Two, I made a logistic curve fit on the global GDP data. It showed the maximum global GDP was 2.12 times the value in 2018. Now it is possible to make a better GDP projection. Using all the equations above, the projection is the maximum global GDP is 2.33 times the value in 2018. Now, it is possible to say with more confidence the maximum global GDP is expected to be about twice the value in 2018 if current trends continue. Graph A.2 below compares the global GDP data to the fits from Chapter Two, this Appendix, and exponential function.

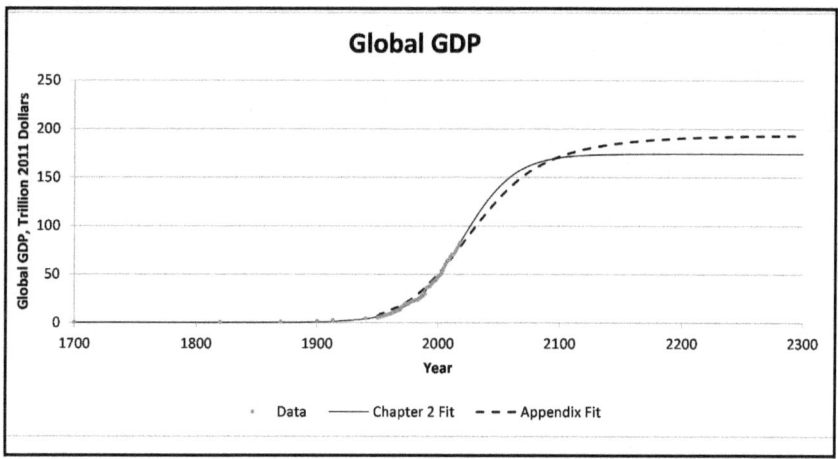

Graph A.2. Global GDP data and Projections

The projection from this appendix results in the continuing of the slowing of growth since the 1960s shown in Table 2.3.

Acknowledgments

There are many people without whose help this book would have been impossible. First and foremost is my wife, Lisa, whose unwavering support lifted me up when the stark reality of the climate crisis and economic inequality got me down. Then there is my daughter Amber Elias who encouraged me to put more of myself into the book and helped with the preface. A friend of mine, Russell England helped with an initial edit. He is a retired marine biologist who spent his career working on river conservation for the State of Georgia and is the author of, *Gross Deceptive Product, An Ecological Perspective on the Economy*. He went through the draft manuscript with a fine toothed comb. He suggested changes and had really good questions and comments that were very helpful. Skyler Perkins at CASSE reviewed the manuscript and provided helpful feedback. Finally, the staff at Dorrance turned the manuscript in a finished book. I am profoundly grateful to all of these people.

NOTES

1. Daly, Herman E. and Farley, Josh. *Ecological Economics: Principles and Applications*, (2nd ed.). Washington, Covelo, and London: Island Press, 2004.

2. Nordhaus, William. Scientific and Economic Background on DICE models. In *William Nordhaus website*. 2017. Retrieved, February 11, 2019 from https://sites.google.com/site/williamdnordhaus/dice-riceco2.

3. Reich, Robert B. *Saving Capitalism: for the many, not the few*. New York: Alfred A. Knopf, 2015.

4. Brown, Lester R. *World on the Edge: How to Prevent Environmental and Economic Collapse*. New York and London: W. W. Norton & Company, 2011.

5. Klein, Naomi. *This Changes Everything: Capitalism vs The Climate*. New York, London, Toronto, Sydney, New Delhi: Simon & Schuster Paperbacks, 2014.

6. "BP Energy Outlook." Retrieved May 14, 2019, from https://www.bp.com/en/global/corporate/energy-economics/energy-outlook.html.

7. "The Penn World Table." Retrieved May 14, 2019, from https://www.rug.nl/ggdc/productivity/pwt/pwt-releases/pwt8.0.

8. "The World Bank, GDP Data," Retrieved May 14, 2019, from https://data.worldbank.org/indicator/ny.gdp.mktp.kd.zg.

9. Wikipedia contributors. (2019, April 3). "Solow–Swan model." *Wikipedia, The Free Encyclopedia*. Retrieved, May 17, 2019, from https://en.wikipedia.org/w/index.php?title=Solow%E2%80%93Swan_model&oldid=890757971.

10. Ortiz-Ospina, Esteban and Tzvetkova, Sandra. "Working women: Key facts and trends in female labor force participation,", In *Our World in Data*, 2017. Retrieved February 10, 2019, from https://ourworldindata.org/female-labor-force-participation-key-facts.

11. Wikipedia contributors. "Sigmoid function." In *Wikipedia, The Free Encyclopedia*, 2018. Retrieved 20:53, February 10, 2019. from https://en.wikipedia.org/w/index.php?title=Sigmoid_function&oldid=874871194.

12. Wikipedia contributors. "Logistic function." In *Wikipedia, The Free Encyclopedia*, 2019. Retrieved 20:54, February 10, 2019, from https://en.wikipedia.org/w/index.php?title=Logistic_function&oldid=880556507.

13. Acemoglu, Daron. *Introduction to Modern Economic Growth*. Princeton and Oxford. Princeton University Press, 2009.

14. United Nations. "World Population to 2300." In *United Nations*, 2004. Retrieved Maay 17, 2019, from https://www.un.org/en/development/desa/population/publications/pdf/trends/WorldPop2300final.pdf.

15. The World Bank, "GDP Data." Retrieved February 10, 2019, from https://data.worldbank.org/indicator/NY.GDP.MKTP.KD.

16. Piketty, Thomas. *Capital in the Twenty-First Century* (Arthur Goldhammer Trans.). Cambridge Massachusetts and London, England.

The Belknap Press of Harvard University Press, 2014.

17.   Colander, Landreth. *History of Economic Thought* (4th ed.). Boston and Toronto: Houghton Mifflin Company, 2002.

18.   Wikipedia contributors. "A rising tide lifts all boats." In *Wikipedia, The Free Encyclopedia*, 2019. Retrieved February 10, 2019, from https://en.wikipedia.org/w/index.php?title=A_rising_tide_lifts_all_boats&oldid=880887294.

19.   Wikipedia contributors. "List of countries by income equality." In *Wikipedia, The Free Encyclopedia*, 2019. Retrieved February 10, 2019, from https://en.wikipedia.org/w/index.php?title=List_of_countries_by_income_equality&oldid=882142628.

20.   Wolf, Connor D. "Why Income Inequality Might Actually Be A Good Thing." *Inside Sources*, 2016. Retrieved February 10, 2019, from https://www.insidesources.com/why-income-inequality-might-actually-be-good/.

21.   Ariely, Dan. "How equal do we want the world to be? You'd be surprised." *TED Talks*, 2015. Retrieved February 10, 2019, from https://www.ted.com/talks/dan_ariely_how_equal_do_we_want_the_world_to_be_you_d_be_surprised.

22.   Greaves, Gerry. "Equality in a post-growth society: Are we ready for tomorrow?" *Post Growth Institute*, 2017. Retrieved February 10, 2019, from http://postgrowth.org/equality-in-a-post-growth-society-are-we-ready-for-tomorrow/.

23.   Wilkinson, Richard and Pickett, Kate. *The Spirit Level: Why Greater Equality Makes Societies Stronger*. New York, London, Oxford, New Delhi and Sydney. Bloomsbury Press, 2011.

24.   O'Neill, Dietz and Jones (eds.). *Enough is Enough: Ideas for a Sustainable Economy in a World of Finite Resources*, 2010. Retrieved May 20, 2019, from http://www.steadystate.org/wp-content/uploads/EnoughIsEnough_FullReport.pdf.

25.   Sapolsky, Robert M. "The Health-Wealth Gap: The growing gulf between rich and poor inflicts biological damage on the bodies and brains." *Scientific American*, Volume 319 (Number 5), 2018.

26.   Boyce, James K. "The Environmental Cost of Inequality: Power imbalances facilitate environmental degradation and the poor suffer the consequences." *Scientific American*, Volume 319 (Number 5), 2018.

27.   Walsh, Brian. "The Triple Whopper Environmental Impact of Global Meat Production." *Time*, 2013. Retrieved February 10, 2019, from http://science.time.com/2013/12/16/the-triple-whopper-environmental-impact-of-global-meat-production/.

28.   Kaneda, Toshiko, and Jason Bremner. "Understanding Population Projections: Assumptions Behind the Numbers." *Population Reference Bureau*, 2014. Retrieved February 10, 2019, from https://www.prb.org/united-nations-population-projections/.

29.   United Nations. "World Population Prospects: Methodology of the United Nations Population Estimates and Projections." *United Nations*, 2017. Retrieved February 10, 2019, from https://population.un.org/wpp/Publications/Files/WPP2017_Methodology.pdf.

30.   Diamond, Jared. *Collapse: How Societies Choose to Fail or Succeed*. New York: Penguin Books, 2011.

31.   Motesharreia, Rivasb, and Kalnay. Human and nature dynamics (HANDY): Modeling inequality and use of resources in the collapse or sustainability of societies. In *Ecological Economics*, 2014. Retrieved February 10, 2019, from https://www.researchgate.net/publication/261291435_Human_and_nature_dynamics_HANDY_Modeling_inequality_and_use_of_resources_in_the_collapse_or_sustainability_of_societies.

32.   Greaves, Gerry. "HANDY.xlsx." *Sustainability Chalkboard*, 2015. Retrieved February 10, 2019, from https://sites.google.com/site/sustainabilitychalkboard/course-materials/links/book-references.

33. Deign, Jason. "2,500 Cities Have Taken Up the Climate-Change Fight." *Green Tech Medi*, 2017. Retrieved May 20, 2019, from https://www.greentechmedia.com/articles/read/how-cities-are-taking-up-the-climate-change-fight#gs.d85e5h.

34. Wikipedia contributors. "Paris Agreement." *Wikipedia, The Free Encyclopedia*, 2019. Retrieved 20:40, May 20, 2019, from https://en.wikipedia.org/w/index.php?title=Paris_Agreement&oldid=896894244.

35. Wikipedia contributors. "Dependency ratio." *Wikipedia, The Free Encyclopedia*, 2019. Retrieved, February 11, 2019, from https://en.wikipedia.org/w/index.php?title=Dependency_ratio&oldid=878712582.

36. Ament, Joe. "The Ecosystem is More Complex Than We May Ever Understand—Our Money System Needn't Be." *Economics for the Anthropocene*, 2016. Retrieved, February 11, 2019, from https://e4a-net.org/2016/10/20/2227/.

37. Wikipedia contributors. "Reserve requirement." *Wikipedia, The Free Encyclopedia*, 2019. Retrieved, February 11, 2019, from https://en.wikipedia.org/w/index.php?title=Reserve_requirement&oldid=878641157.

38. Wikipedia contributors. "Market liquidity." *Wikipedia, The Free Encyclopedia*, 2019. Retrieved 14:38, February 11, 2019, from https://en.wikipedia.org/w/index.php?title=Market_liquidity&oldid=879891714.

39. Wikipedia contributors. "Stimulus (economics)." *Wikipedia, The Free Encyclopedia*, 2018. Retrieved, February 11, 2019, from https://en.wikipedia.org/w/index.php?title=Stimulus_(economics)&oldid=874524941.

40. Knoop, Todd A. *Business Cycle Economics: Understanding Recessions and the Depressions from Boom to Bust.* Santa Barbara, Denver and Oxford: Praeger, 2015.

41. Wikipedia contributors. "Gross domestic product." *Wikipedia, The Free Encyclopedia*, 2019. Retrieved, February 11, 2019, from https://en.wikipedia.org/w/index.php?title=Gross_domestic_product&oldid=882782974.

42. Rogers, Simon. "Bobby Kennedy on GDP: 'measures everything except that which is worthwhile.'" *The Guardian*, 2012. Retrieved, February 11, 2019, from https://www.theguardian.com/news/datablog/2012/may/24/robert-kennedy-gdp.

43. Wikipedia contributors. "Human Development Index."*Wikipedia, The Free Encyclopedia*, 2019. Retrieved, February 11, 2019, from https://en.wikipedia.org/w/index.php?title=Human_Development_Index&oldid=882720897.

44. Wikipedia contributors. "Genuine progress indicator." *Wikipedia, The Free Encyclopedia*, 2019. Retrieved, February 11, 2019, from https://en.wikipedia.org/w/index.php?title=Genuine_progress_indicator&oldid=882310867.

45. Wikipedia contributors. "Campaign finance reform in the United States." In *Wikipedia, The Free Encyclopedia*, 2019. Retrieved, February 11, 2019, from https://en.wikipedia.org/w/index.php?title=Campaign-_finance_reform_in_the_United_States&oldid=876588704.

46. Wikipedia contributors. "Campaign finance in the United States." *Wikipedia, The Free Encyclopedia*, 2019. Retrieved, February 11, 2019, from https://en.wikipedia.org/w/index.php?title=Campaign_finance_in_the_United_States&oldid=876588903.

47. Ackerman, Bruce and Ian Ayres. *Voting with Dollars: A New Paradigm for Campaign Finance*. New Haven & London: Yale University Press, 2004.

48. Ackerman, Bruce and Ian Ayres. "Democracy dollars can give every voter a real voice in American politics." In *The Washington Post*, 2015. Retrieved, February 11, 2019, from https://www.washingtonpost.com/opinions/democracy-dollars-can-give-every-voter-a-real-voice-in-american-politics/2015/11/05/48100ae8-8345-11e5-a7ca-6ab6ec20f839_story.html?utm_term=.26c1575ad8ca.

49. Levine, Bertram J. and Michael Johnston. "Campaign contributions should be anonymous." In *The Washington Post*, 2014. Retrieved, February 11, 2019, from https://www.washingtonpost.com/opinions/making-campaign-contributions-anonymous/2014/09/04/65f2b8d8-2e39-11e4-9b98-848790384093_story.html?utm_term=.74d870fe6fe6.

50. Open Secrets. Bernie Sanders. In *Open Secrets: Center for Responsive Politics*, 2016. Retrieved, February 11, 2019, from https://www.opensecrets.org/pres16/candidate.php?id=N00000528.

51. Open Secrets. Beto O'Rourke. In *Open Secrets: Center for Responsive Politics*, 2016. Retrieved, February 11, 2019, from https://www.opensecrets.org/members-of-congress/summary?cid=N00033540.

52. Balk, Gene. "Do Seattle's democracy vouchers work? New analysis says yes." *The Seattle Times*, 2017. Retrieved, February 11, 2019, from https://www.seattletimes.com/seattle-news/data/do-seattles-democracy-vouchers-work-new-analysis-says-yes/.

53. Duchin, Moon. "Mathematicians are Developing Forensics to Identify Political Maps that Disenfranchise Voters, Geometry v. Gerrymandering." *Scientific American*, Volume 319 (Number 5), 2018.

54. Krishnan, Chandu. "Fixing the Revolving Door." *Harvard, Edmond J. Safra Center for Ethics*, 2014. Retrieved, February 11, 2019, from https://ethics.harvard.edu/blog/fixing-revolving-door.

55. Wikipedia contributors. "Paris Agreement." In *Wikipedia, The Free Encyclopedia*, 2019. Retrieved, February 11, 2019, from https://en.wikipedia.org/w/index.php?title=Paris_Agreement&oldid=882275756.

56. Nordhaus, William. "Scientific and Economic Background on DICE models." *William Nordhaus website*, 2017. Retrieved, February 11, 2019, from https://sites.google.com/site/williamdnordhaus/dice-rice.

57. Nordhaus, William. *The Climate Casino: Risk, Uncertainty, and Economics for a Warming World*. New Haven and London: Yale University Press, 2013.

58. Rezai, Armon and Frederick van der Ploeg. *Abandoning Fossil Fuel: How Fast and How Much?*, 2017. Retrieved, May 24, 2019, from https://www.economics.ox.ac.uk/materials/OxCarre/ResearchPapers/OxCarreRP2013123.pdf.

59. Weitzman, Martin L. *What is the "damages function" for global warming – and what difference might it make?*, 2010. Retrieved, May 24, 2019, from https://scholar.harvard.edu/weitzman/files/damagesfunction-globalwarming.pdf.

60. Ackerman, F. and Elizabeth A. Stanton. *Climate risks and carbon prices: revising the social cost of carbon. Economics,* The Open-Access, Open-Assessment E-Journal, 6, 2012-10. Retrieved, May 24, 2019, from http://www.decarboni.se/sites/default/files/publications/51261/economics-2012-10.pdf.

61. Oil Change International. "Fossil Fuel Subsidies: Overview." *Oil Change International*, 2017. Retrieved, February 11, 2019, from http://priceofoil.org/fossil-fuel-subsidies/.

62. Wikipedia contributors. "G20." *Wikipedia, The Free Encyclopedia*, 2019. Retrieved, February 11, 2019, from https://en.wikipedia.org/w/index.php?title=G20&oldid=882782417.

63. Greaves, Gerry. "Equality in a post-growth society: Are we ready for tomorrow?" In *Post Growth Institute*, 2017. Retrieved February 10, 2019, from http://postgrowth.org/equality-in-a-post-growth-society-are-we-ready-for-tomorrow/.

64. Wikipedia contributors. "Estate tax in the United States." *Wikipedia, The Free Encyclopedia*, 2019. Retrieved, February 11, 2019, from https://en.wikipedia.org/w/index.php?title=Estate_tax_in_the_United_States&oldid=882677864.

65. Jacobson, Raub, and Johnson. The Estate Tax: Ninety Years and Counting. In *Internal Revenue Service*, 2016. Retrieved, February 11, 2019, from https://www.irs.gov/pub/irs-soi/ninetyestate.pdf.

66. Mayer, Jane. *Dark Money: The Hidden History of the Billionaires Behind the Rise of the Radical Right.* New York, London, Toronto, Sydney, Auckland: Doubleday, 2016.

67. Wikipedia contributors. "Economic mobility." *Wikipedia, The Free Encyclopedia*, 2019. Retrieved, February 11, 2019, from https://en.wikipedia.org/w/index.php?title=Economic_mobility&oldid=882683411.

68. Orem, Tina. "2018-2019 Gift Tax Rates: I'm Generous, but Do I Have to Pay This? Two things keep the IRS' hands out of most people's financial candy dish: the annual gift tax exclusion and the lifetime exclusion." *Nerdwallet*, 2019. Retrieved, February 11, 2019, from https://www.nerdwallet.com/blog/taxes/gift-tax-rate/.

69. Wikipedia contributors. "Basic income around the world." *Wikipedia, The Free Encyclopedia*, 2019. Retrieved, February 11, 2019, from https://en.wikipedia.org/w/index.php?title=Basic_income_around_the_world&oldid=881095576.

70. Worldwatch Institute. "Agricultural Subsidies Remain a Staple in the Industrial World." *Worldwatch Institute*, 2014. Retrieved, February 11, 2019, from http://www.worldwatch.org/agricultural-subsidies-remain-staple-industrial-world-0.

71. Kliff, Sarah. "The true story of America's sky-high prescription drug prices." *Vox*, 2018. Retrieved, February 11, 2019, from https://www.vox.com/science-and-health/2016/11/30/12945756/prescription-drug-prices-explained.

72. Scott, Dylan. "The untold story of TV's first prescription drug ad." *Stat News*, 2015. Retrieved, February 11, 2019, from https://www.statnews.com/2015/12/11/untold-story-tvs-first-prescription-drug-ad/.

73. Collins, Mike. "The Big Bank Bailout." *Forbes*, 2015. Retrieved, February 11, 2019, from https://www.forbes.com/sites/mikecollins/2015/07/14/the-big-bank-bailout/#154c6ba12d83.

74. "Dr. Econ." "Why did the Federal Reserve start paying interest on reserve balances held on deposit at the Fed? Does the Fed pay interest on required reserves, excess reserves, or both? What interest rate does the Fed pay?" *Federal Reserve Bank of San Francisco*, 2013. Retrieved, February 11, 2019, from https://www.frbsf.org/education/publications/doctor-econ/2013/march/federal-reserve-interest-balances-reserves/.

75. Chen, Han and Danielle Droitsch. "Time for the US to End Fossil Fuel Subsidies." *Natural Resources Defense Council*, 2018. Retrieved, February 11, 2019, from https://www.nrdc.org/experts/danielle-droitsch/time-us-end-fossil-fuel-subsidies.

76. National Sustainable Agriculture Coalition. Organization home page. Retrieved, February 11, 2019, from http://sustainableagriculture.net/.

77. Holtz-Eakin, Douglas. "The Drug Pricing Reform Effort." *American Action Forum*, 2018. Retrieved, February 12, 2019, from https://www.americanactionforum.org/daily-dish/drug-pricing-reform-effort/.

78. Wikipedia contributors. "Prescription drug prices in the United States." *Wikipedia, The Free Encyclopedia*, 2019. Retrieved, February 12, 2019, from https://en.wikipedia.org/w/index.php?title=Prescription_drug_prices_in_the_United_States&oldid=882192463.

79. Brannon, Ike and Elizabeth Lowell. "Export-Import Bank: Obstacles and Options for Reform." *American Action Forum*, 2011. Retrieved, February 12, 2019, from https://www.americanactionforum.org/wp-content/uploads/sites/default/files/Ex-Im%20Final%20Draft21.pdf.

80. *American Action Forum*. Retrieved, February 12, 2019, from https://www.americanactionforum.org/search-form/?search=export+import+credit&dd=on&mdy=&aut_ids=&engine=default&stype=advanced.

81. Bernstein, Jared. "Do not go gently into that financial regulatory roll-

back." *The Washington Post*, 2018. Retrieved, February 12, 2019, from https://www.washingtonpost.com/news/posteverything/wp/2018/06/0 3/do-not-go-gently-into-that-financial-regulatory-rollback/?utm_term=.99b3a12f44ae.

82. Wikipedia contributors. "Gilded Age." In *Wikipedia, The Free Encyclopedia*, 2019. Retrieved, February 12, 2019, from https://en.wikipedia.org/w/index.php?title=Gilded_Age&oldid=881418034.

83. Sahadi, Jeanne. "The richest 10% hold 76% of the wealth." *CNN Money*, 2016. Retrieved, February 12, 2019, from https://money.cnn.com/2016/08/18/pf/wealth-inequality/index.html.

84. Paywizard. "US Federal, States, Cities, Territorial Minimum Wages." Retrieved, February 12, 2019, from https://paywizard.org/salary/minimum-wage.

85. Wikipedia contributors. "Minimum wage in the United States." *Wikipedia, The Free Encyclopedia*, 2019. Retrieved, February 12, 2019, from https://en.wikipedia.org/w/index.php?title=Minimum_wage_in_t he_United_States&oldid=882774223.

86. Dube, Arindrajit. "Designing Thoughtful Minimum Wage Policy at the State and Local Levels." *The Brooking's Institution*. Retrieved, February 12, 2019, from https://www.brookings.edu/wp-content/uploads-/2016/06/state_local_minimum_wage_policy_dube.pdf.

87. Wikipedia contributors. "Absolute advantage." *Wikipedia, The Free Encyclopedia*, 2018. Retrieved, February 12, 2019, from https://en.wikipedia.org/w/index.php?title=Absolute_advantage&oldid=870527142.

88. Wikipedia contributors. "Comparative advantage." *Wikipedia, The Free Encyclopedia*, 2019. Retrieved, February 12, 2019, from https://en.wikipedia.org/w/index.php?title=Comparative_advantage&oldid=877460634.

89. Stiglitz, Joseph E. "A Rigged Economy: And what we can do about it." *Scientific American*, Volume 319 (Number 5), 2018.

90. Wikipedia contributors. "Income tax in the United States." *Wikipedia, The Free Encyclopedia*, 2019. Retrieved, February 12, 2019, from https://en.wikipedia.org/w/index.php?title=Income_tax_in_the_ United_States&oldid=881107312.

91. The Tax Foundation. "Federal Individual Income Tax Rates History." *The Tax Foundation*. Retrieved, February 12, 2019, from https://files.taxfoundation.org/legacy/docs/fed_individual_rate_h istory_nominal.pdf.

92. "File:Historical Marginal Tax Rate for Highest and Lowest Income Earners.jpg." *Wikimedia Commons, the free media repository*, 2017. Retrieved, February 12, 2019 from https://commons.wikimedia.org/w/index.php?title=File:Historic- al_Marginal_Tax_Rate_for_Highest_and_Lowest_Income_Earners.jpg &oldid=238666700.

93. Chu, Ben. "Global debt: Why has it hit an all-time high? And how worried should we be about it? Who has all this debt? Who is it owed to? What does this level of indebtedness mean?" *Independent*, 2018. Retrieved, February 12, 2019 from https://www.independent.co.uk/news/business/analysis-and- features/global-debt-crisis-explained-all-time-high-world-economy- causes-solutions-definition-a8143516.html.

94. Amadeo, Kimberly. "2008 Financial Crisis Timeline: 37 Critical Events in the Worst Crisis Since the Depression." *the balance*, 2019. Retrieved, February 12, 2019 from https://www.thebalance.com/2008- financial-crisis-timeline-3305540.

95. Leaders. "The next capitalist revolution." *The Economist*, 2018.

96. Wikipedia contributors. "Glass–Steagall legislation." In *Wikipedia, The Free Encyclopedia*, 2019. Retrieved, February 12, 2019, from https://en.wikipedia.org/w/index.php?title=Glass%E2%80%93S teagall_legislation&oldid=879653371.

97. Wikipedia contributors. "Commercial bank." *Wikipedia, The Free*

Encyclopedia, 2019. Retrieved, February 12, 2019, from https://en.wikipedia.org/w/index.php?title=Commercial_bank&oldid=880900857.

98. Wikipedia contributors. "Investment banking." *Wikipedia, The Free Encyclopedia*, 2019. Retrieved, February 12, 2019, from https://en.wikipedia.org/w/index.php?title=Investment_banking&oldid=881549982

99. Federal Reserve System. "Purpose: Overview of the Federal Reserve System. The Federal Reserve performs five key functions in the public interest to promote the health of the U.S. economy and the stability of the U.S. financial system." *Federal Reserve*. Retrieved, February 12, 2019, from https://www.federalreserve.gov/aboutthefed/files/pf_1.pdf.

100. Wikipedia contributors. "Fractional-reserve banking." *Wikipedia, The Free Encyclopedia*, 2018. Retrieved, February 12, 2019, from https://en.wikipedia.org/w/index.php?title=Fractional-reserve_banking&oldid=874307634.

101. Carlson, Mark. "Lessons from the Historical Use of Reserve Requirements in the United States to Promote Bank Liquidity. The Federal Reserve, 2013. Retrieved, February 12, 2019, from https://www.federalreserve.gov/pubs/feds/2013/201311/201311pap.pdf.

102. Federal Reserve System. "Reserve Requirements." In the Federal Reserve, 2018 Retrieved, February 12, 2019, from https://www.federalreserve.gov/monetarypolicy/reservereq.htm.

103. Jackson, Tim. "Prosperity Without Growth? The transition to a sustainable economy." *Sustainable Development Commission*, 2019. Retrieved, February 12, 2019, from http://www.sd-commission.org.uk/data/files/publications/prosperity_without_growth_report.pdf.

104. Hawken, Paul. "Beyond GDP: are there better ways to measure well-being?" *The Conversation*. Retrieved, February 12, 2019, from https://theconversation.com/beyond-gdp-are-there-better-ways-to-measure-well-being-33414.

105. Daly, Lew and Posner, Stephen. "Beyond GDP: New Measures for a New Economy." *Dēmos*, 2011. Retrieved, February 12, 2019, from https://www.demos.org/sites/default/files/publications/BeyondGDP_0.pdf.

106. Wikipedia contributors. "One-child policy." *Wikipedia, The Free Encyclopedia*, 2019. Retrieved, February 12, 2019, from https://en.wikipedia.org/w/index.php?title=One-child_policy&oldid=882515108.

107. Wikipedia contributors. "Demographics of India." *Wikipedia, The Free Encyclopedia*, 2019. Retrieved, February 12, 2019, from https://en.wikipedia.org/w/index.php?title=Demographics_of_India&oldid=882364993.

108. Wikipedia contributors. "Demographics of Africa." In *Wikipedia, The Free Encyclopedia*, 2019. Retrieved, February 12, 2019, from https://en.wikipedia.org/w/index.php?title=Demographics_of_Africa&oldid=882538721.

109. Wikipedia contributors. "Projections of population growth." *Wikipedia, The Free Encyclopedia*, 2019. Retrieved, February 12, 2019, from https://en.wikipedia.org/w/index.php?title=Projections_of_population_growth&oldid=882641455.

110. Kiva.org website. Retrieved, February 12, 2019, from www.kiva.org.

111. Czech, Brain. *Supply Shock: Economic Growth at the Crossroads and the Steady State Economy*. Gabriola Island, Canada: New Society Publishers, 2013.

112. Wikipedia contributors. "Humphrey–Hawkins Full Employment Act." *Wikipedia, The Free Encyclopedia*, 2019. Retrieved 13:05, June 3, 2019, from https://en.wikipedia.org/w/index.php?title=Humphrey%E2%80%93Hawkins_Full_Employment_Act&oldid=888601729.

113. Free Exchange. "Why Americans and Britons work such long hours: Society as a whole must judge whether or not there is more to life than work." *The Economist*, 2018.

114. Jones, Bradley. "Most Americans want to limit campaign spending, say big donors have greater political influence." *Pew Research Center*, 2018. Retrieved, February 12, 2019, from http://www.pewresearch.org/fact-tank/2018/05/08/most-americans-want-to-limit-campaign-spending-say-big-donors-have-greater-political-influence/.

115. Sherman, Rik. "New Poll Shows Most U.S. Voters Think Man-Made Climate Change Is Real." *Forbes*, 2018. Retrieved, February 12, 2019, from http://fortune.com/2018/12/06/poll-climate-change-trump/.

116. Manchester, Julia. "Pollster says most Americans believe economy is rigged to favor the elites." *The Hill*, 2018. Retrieved, February 12, 2019, from https://thehill.com/hilltv/what-americas-thinking/422104-pollster-says-most-americans-believe-the-economy-is-rigged-in.

117. Pew Research Center. "Top voting issues in 2016 election." *Pew Research Center*, 2016. Retrieved, February 12, 2019, from http://www.people-press.org/2016/07/07/4-top-voting-issues-in-2016-election/.

118. Levitsky, Steven and Ziblatt, Daniel. *How Democracies Die*. New York: Crown Publishing Group, 2018.

119. Longley, Robert. "Tips for Writing Effective Letters to Congress." *ThoughtCo.*, 2018. Retrieved, February 13, 2019, from https://www.thoughtco.com/write-effective-letters-to-congress-3322301.

120. Moore, Carter. "Does writing your congressman or senator really do any good, or is it merely a diversionary smokescreen to make the average citizen believe that they have some voice in the legislative process?" *Quora*, 2014. https://www.quora.com/Does-writing-your-congressman-or-senator-really-do-any-good-or-is-it-merely-a-diversionary-smokescreen-to-make-the-average-citizen-believe-that-they-have-some-voice-in-the-l egislative-process.

121. Climate Reality Project website. Retrieved, February 13, 2019, from https://www.climaterealityproject.org/.

122. Kiva.org website. Retrieved, February 13, 2019, from www.kiva.org.

123. Center for the Advancement of the Steady State Economy website. Retrieved, February 13, 2019, from https://steadystate.org/.

124. Greaves, Gerry. "Energy, Climate Change and the Economy." *Post Growth Institute*, 2015. Retrieved February 10, 2019, from http://post-growth.org/energy-climate-change-and-the-economy/.

125. Greaves, Gerry. "Equality in a post-growth society: Are we ready for tomorrow?" *Post Growth Institute*, 2017. Retrieved February 10, 2019, from http://postgrowth.org/equality-in-a-post-growth-society-are-we-ready-for-tomorrow/.

126. Fighting Inequality Alliance website. Retrieved February 10, 2019, from https://www.fightinequality.org/.

127. The Center for Economic and Social Rights website. Retrieved February 10, 2019, from http://www.cesr.org/.

128. Inequality.org website. Retrieved February 10, 2019, from https://inequality.org/

129. United Nations. "World Population Prospects." *United Nations*, 2019. Retrieved July 17, 2019, from https://population.un.org/wpp/Download/Probabilistic/Population/_

130. Climate Action Tracker. "Conceptualizing the Paris Agreement long-term temperature goal." Retrieved July 17, 2019, from https://climateactiontracker.org/methodology/paris-temperature-goal/.

131. Wikipedia contributors. "List of regions by past GDP (PPP)." *Wikipedia, The Free Encyclopedia*, 2019/ Retrieved 11:02, August 14, 2019, from https://en.wikipedia.org/w/index.php?title=List_of_regions_by_past_GDP_(PPP)&oldid=904762267

ABOUT THE AUTHOR

I am a retired engineer with a BS in Civil Engineering including an emphasis on structural analysis from the University of Rhode Island 1975. While in school, I read the Club of Rome report, *Limits to Growth*, which made sense to me. I considered emphasizing environmental engineering, but ultimately structural analysis spoke to me. I spent the next thirty-nine years as a structural engineer mostly in a Research and Development environment. I developed a reputation as an excellent problem solver, often in areas where I was not an expert or even knowledgeable. Over the years, ideas from *Limits to Growth* had been fermenting in the background. In the year 2000, I began my climate change journey. I was working as an engineer on the energy saving effects of cool roofs for building energy standards. Soon the discussion changed to the effect of cool roofs on climate change. I didn't know much about climate change, so I did some digging. I came to three conclusions: climate change was real, we were causing it by emitting CO_2 from the burning of fossil fuels, and the effects, while uncertain, were very bad. I started focusing on improving the energy efficiency of homes including developing cost effective zero energy homes. This led to evaluations of the effects of efficiency improvements on climate change and the conclusion while efficiency improvements can help significantly, they are not enough. In 2007, I started working in our company's sustainability organization where I found energy use is inextricably linked to the size of our economy as measured by GDP. I retired in 2014.

Of course, there were several considerations in my decision to retire, but one of them was to have more time to explore the connection between climate change and the economy. In retirement, I have been working on the economics of low or no growth and am particularly concerned with inequality and our ability to manage the stability of the economic/financial system in low growth scenarios. I am the Director of the Upstate South Carolina Chapter of the Center for the Advancement of the Steady State Economy and have written blogs for the Post Growth Institute. I have also completed the Climate Reality Project Leadership Training in March 2019. All this ultimately led to this book.

INDEX